Praise for *We, me, them & it,*
the previous book by John Simmons

'For weeks, the book rested with many others, then something intrigued me about the title. I read it in one sitting. Fascinating.'
Niall FitzGerald, Chairman, Unilever

'A rarity in the world of business books: something readable, stimulating and full of good sense . . . Simmons makes a heartfelt plea for plain English, and encourages us to harness the power of words to tell stories, embody corporate ideals, and help to create brands.'
Book of the Week, *Marketing* magazine

'A stimulating and thought-provoking journey.'
Jon Potter, Global Brand Director of Guinness

'*We, me, them & it* is a spirited, smart book about how to write at work.'
Jacqueline Blais, *USA Today*

'Simmons, one of the world's top business creative writers, believes "Words can move, explain, startle, persuade, express ideas . . . and more." And the man is out to convince you of this. This book is sure to prove inspiring to all businessmen.'
The month's best ink, *FHM* magazine

'What a pleasure it was to read *We, me, them & it*. As I can keep impressing on our economists here, it is no use having a good idea if you cannot communicate it to someone else. The power and joy of words you certainly did communicate in the book. Its lessons will not be forgotten, at least in the Bank.'
Mervyn King, Governor-Elect, Bank of England

*The invisible grail*

# THE
# INVISIBLE
# GRAIL

**In search of the true language of brands**

## John Simmons

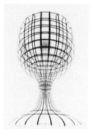

TEXERE

Copyright © 2003 John Simmons

Published in 2003 by

TEXERE Publishing Limited
71–77 Leadenhall Street
London EC3A 3DE

Tel +44 (0)20 7204 3644
Fax +44 (0)20 7208 6701
www.etexere.co.uk

A subsidiary of

TEXERE LLC
55 East 52nd Street
New York, NY 10055

Tel +1 (212) 317 5511
Fax +1 (212) 317 5178
www.etexere.com

The right of John Simmons to be identified as the author of this work has been asserted by him in accordance with the Copyright, Designs and Patents Act 1988.

All rights reserved.

No part of this publication may be reproduced, stored in a retrieval system or transmitted in any form or by any means including photocopying, electronic, mechanical, recording or otherwise, without the prior written permission of the right holders, application for which must be made to the publisher.

No responsibility can be accepted by the publisher for action taken as a result of information contained in this publication. Readers should take specific advice when dealing with specific situations.

TEXERE books may be purchased for educational, business, or sales promotional use. For more information please write to the Special Markets Department at the TEXERE London or New York address.

Design by David Carroll. Artwork by Nicholas Wright. Cover illustration by Karim Borhanuddin.

A CIP catalogue record for this book is available from the British Library.

ISBN 1-58799-156-X

Printed and bound in Great Britain by Biddles Ltd. Jacket printed by Westerham Press.

This book is printed on acid free paper responsibly manufactured from sustainable forestry, in which at least two trees are planted for each one used for paper production.

10 9 8 7 6 5 4 3 2 1

*For Mike Fosbrook*
*1947–2002*
*Friend and writer*

# Thank you

All books are created by many people, even if there is only a single writer. Many people inspired the writing of this book, in particular by responding to my previous book *We, me, them & it*. I'm particularly grateful to those readers who took the trouble to review that book enthusiastically on the Amazon site.

*The invisible grail* was written outside working hours but was, of course, informed by my daily work at Interbrand. I'm grateful to my colleagues Mark Griffiths and Katriona Campbell who read and commented on the chapters as I wrote them. Rita Clifton gave me every encouragement to keep writing. Many clients gave me advice, permission and enthusiasm to write their stories: Jon Potter of Guinness; John Dodds of Air Products; David May of the BBC; Alastair Creamer and Steve Miles of Unilever; David Powell of the Bank of Ireland; David Croom of Nelson Croom.

There were a number of people whom I met through writing case studies for this book. It was a wonderful bonus to me that Richard Reed and Dan Germain of Innocent Drinks, Sarah McCartney of Lush and Mike Harris of Egg all turned out to be every bit as stimulating as the brands they have done so much to create through their words. I thank them for being so open and honest with me and their customers.

I would like to mention Sarah Isles and Penny Egan of the Royal Society of Arts, who invited me to give the keynote talk on 'World Speak: English as a global language?' at an RSA conference in March 2001. That proved a spur to much of the research and thinking in Chapter 2 of this book.

During the period of this book's genesis I had the amazing experience of being a writer-in-residence for six months at Lever Fabergé. My fellow writer-in-residence was the poet Jackie Wills, who taught me so much and reawakened my imagination to many new kinds of poetry and writing.

David Wilson and Myles Thompson have been sources of encouragement at my publisher TEXERE. David, in particular, took the book from its earliest idea and barest description, and seemed to understand it in its final form even before I had written a word in earnest. The most precious gift a writer can receive is encouragement and I received lots of this from David, his predecessor Martin Liu, and the team at TEXERE.

David Carroll again labored hard and long to design the book with flair and attention to detail. I believe absolutely that written words are enhanced by the skill of a designer. David has been not just a great designer but a good friend.

Finally, as ever, my love and thanks go to Linda who gave me all the support I could have wished for. Without her, and without Matthew and Jessie (who took most of the photos), there would have been no book at all.

# Contents

Grail (in full Holy Grail) is an object of quest in medieval legend. The grail is supposed to be the chalice from which Christ drank at the Last Supper or the cup in which Joseph of Arimathea caught the blood of the crucified Christ. It was believed that, if discovered, it would confer mystical benefits on the discoverer. In the Arthurian cycle of legends it became a symbol of perfection sought by the Knights of the Round Table.

'Then there entered into the hall the Holy Grail, covered with white samite, but there was none might see it nor who have it. And there was the hall fulfilled with good odors, and every knight had such meats and drinks as he best loved in this world. And when the Holy Grail had been borne through the hall, then the holy vessel departed suddenly, that they wist not where it became.'
Thomas Malory, *La queste del Saint Graal*

'He used to run as if the Holy Grail were just around the corner, and he might catch it if only he could run fast enough.'
HW Nevinson

'We have all seen
The moon in lonely alleys make
A grail of laughter of an empty ash can.'
Hart Crane, *Chaplinesque*

'With the sextant he made obeisance to the sun-god, he consulted ancient tomes and tables of magic characters, muttered prayers in a strange tongue that sounded like Indexerrorparallaxrefraction, made cabalistic signs on paper, added and carried one, and then, on a piece of holy script called the Grail – I mean, the Chart – he placed his finger on a certain space conspicuous for its blankness and said, 'Here we are.' When we looked at

the blank space and asked, "And where is that?" he answered in the cipher-code of the higher priesthood, "31 – 15 – 47 north, 133 – 5 – 30 west." And we said "Oh", and felt mighty small.'
Jack London, *The cruise of the Snark*


'He had intended, probably, to take what he could and go – but now he found that he had committed himself to the following of a grail.'
F Scott Fitzgerald, *The Great Gatsby*


*Mulder:* That isn't the real Shroud of Turin, is it?
*Scully:* No, Agent Mulder. Just a replica. I keep the original in the basement, next to the Holy Grail.
*The X-Files*

**Setting out** *'If you should write a fable for little fishes, you would make them speak like great whales.'*
Goldsmith to Johnson, quoted in *Moby Dick*
by Herman Melville

# The quest

The basic narrative of this book is the quest for the 'grail' that will enable brands to build better relationships with their audiences. Brands want customers, in particular, to love them. But brands are discovering too that their own employees are customers who cannot be ignored. In searching for this kind of affection, brands are seeking a level of commitment, based on trust and loyalty, both from customers and employees.

They seek affection because few have it. The world's biggest brands are immensely well recognized but not always well loved. Can the world's biggest brands learn from smaller brands about ways to build deeper relationships with audiences? And if we all use words in everyday life to build relationships, how well do brands use words in their business communications? Are there parallels there that will inform our quest?

We will seek answers to those questions, and the process of seeking will guide our journey. The reward will be great for if we succeed we will reveal a force that can give new life to brands. At the moment it is unseen but we know that, if it is to give life, it must be a creative force. We will use words to pursue our quest, with the suspicion that words themselves might also hold the secret to the quest. Because words are a creative force: words that write poems, tell jokes, engage people in conversations. Words that tell stories.

There is conflict too. Quest, love, conflict. The grand themes of storytelling are powerful simply because they are embedded in all our lives, including our business lives.

The events of September 11 2001 inevitably made us see the world in terms of conflict, but the language of confrontation had ruled for a long time before then.

Business generally needs little encouragement to unfurl the flag of military metaphor. Companies are always keen to use competitive weapons. That quintessential word of management thinking – 'strategy' – derives from Greek words for leading an army. We slash prices, wage war on waste, fight for market share. But the language has intensified in recent years as business has lost stability. Business loses confidence in times of recession and starts to compete with a sharper edge of aggression. Companies become less inclined to take risks, and the safe option is to use words that show how tough you really are. Recessionary times bring on regressionary language, with marketing people retreating to playground shouting for attention instead of engaging in adult conversation. Sectors of business that once encouraged the most chivalrous of approaches now witness the equivalent of hand-to-hand scrapping for territory. Think of airlines, for example.

In effect, a war is being fought, a war of words. But there is also guerrilla warfare going on, where one side has the power of a simple slogan 'No logo', and the other side has not yet marshaled its arguments to make an equally effective counter attack. Naomi Klein has led the rebellion against what she sees as all-powerful, frequently immoral, global brands. These brands have been identified as the villains, as symbols of unaccountable capitalism, by anarchist protestors worldwide. The protestors' strategy inevitably involves violence.

Under attack, the brands have lost some confidence and gone into retreat. They have become more aware that gaps have opened between their view of the world and the view of many of their potential customers. But they are not properly equipped to move quickly towards a language of cooperation and connection. The words are lacking.

Having taken words for granted during the years of big brand ascendancy, or having used them as weapons of domination, businesses now find themselves in a situation that calls for a different approach. Words into ploughshares, swords into pens. Businesses now need to build brands that go beyond a simplistic reliance on the heavy artillery of logos and advertising, because there is a subtler campaign to be fought. Brands are looking for what seems to be a holy grail – the holy grail of customer commitment and affection. But how do you discover this? Should you use words – and use them more creatively, effectively, engagingly?

Ah, there's the rub. When it comes to the big brands, they've organized themselves out of the ability to be light and engaging with words, they've come to see words as a fairly standard business tool, a necessary but unexciting evil. They give very little credit to words. They pay little attention to the ability of their leaders and managers to use words. It is not surprising that these managers neglect the potential of language as they seek to build brands that are more clearly differentiated. It is simply not seen by them as an important issue. It is outside what they are taught, beyond their normal sphere of understanding. It is invisible in effect.

So already we have our first clue that will help us in our quest. Brands might need to be more creative in their use of language, not in their advertising but in every area of internal and external communication. Brands need to discover or rediscover the power of words to help them connect more emotionally with consumers, with all audiences. The means to do this is through verbal identity, which enables brands to use names, expressive language, conversations, narrative, storytelling, as consistently and emotively as they have previously used visual identity (logos, symbols, colors, graphics).

Last year I read Ruth L Oseki's wonderful novel *My year of meat*. The main character's Japanese mother said something that appealed to me a lot.

**How can you say 'just a name'? Name is very first thing. Name is face to all the world.**

In the context of a brand – and what I call verbal identity – the name is undoubtedly first thing and it is the face to all the world. So, in the prologue to our journey, let me take a name as a starting point for our exploration. And, given that I have referred to Naomi Klein as part of the background, let me take as an example a brand that features as a villain in her book, *No logo*. Starbucks.

Starbucks has spread to every part of the world, as if taking its lead from the character in *Moby Dick* who gives the company its name, sailing the seven seas in pursuit of glory. There is real resonance in the name, evoking the story of the hunt for the great white whale, sea songs and Captain Ahab. But, curiously, Starbucks makes no use of the deeper story that gave it original meaning. Its name remains just a façade, not even a face, and it could have been so much more.

The Naomi Klein case against Starbucks is that behind its New Age appearance hides a capitalist predator, forcing small independent competitors out of business. By 'clustering' – saturating an area with its coffee shops – Starbucks achieves brand dominance and keeps the market comfortably and unfairly to itself. Which means that when you and I want a cup of real coffee from a real family business, we can't have it because Starbucks will have gobbled it up.

I might have more sympathy with the argument if I liked the product less. But the fact is that Starbucks makes coffee that I like. A double espresso with a granola bar, with the morning paper, is as relaxed a start to the day as I've found. There is an enormous new market for coffee-drinking, and it has been created largely by Starbucks. It's hard to criticize Starbucks for killing off the competition when the competition is still out there and thriving. As compared to a handful of independent coffee shops, which you had to seek out with determination, there is now a coffee shop on every corner. And the coffee shops are Starbucks, competitive chains *and* independents. Along the way this development has also had the effect of bringing new life back to high streets that had been in decline, by improving the overall quality of the shopping experience.

Starbucks suffered at the hands of anti-capitalist protestors because it was the biggest and the most ambitious – and therefore a symbol. It was a surprise to me, for example, to find Starbucks in Beijing, intruding into the Forbidden City. As were McDonald's and KFC (with a multi-level restaurant). The argument against this is largely on the grounds of cultural imperialism, an argument I have some sympathy with. Brands have to adapt to local markets, not just impose themselves on them.

There is, however, an important point to bear in mind. What people in Beijing or Moscow are buying is not just a latte or a Big Mac but a brief excursion into America and the luxury that is seen to be American. This is at the root of those brands' popularity, the reason why they have been able to spread globally. In buying the brand people recognize that it contains an element of America – and for millions of people around the world that is still something to aspire to. Other brands have other cultural influences, but the global protestors complain less about the Italianness of Illy, for example, or the Australianness of Foster's. Even when we're told that by drinking Australian, we'll be thinking Australian.

The problem with Starbucks, I believe, is that it has not quite realized the potential of its story. Howard Schultz, the brand's driving force, does much to use his own story – the quintessentially American rags to riches story of the boy from the projects getting to the top through his own strength of character. This suggests one kind of adventurous narrative; then there are the almost mythological associations that could come from *Moby Dick* and the whole idea of adventurous narrative; but also, and perhaps more importantly, the links that the company naturally makes with the people and countries responsible for growing its coffee. Recent moves by Starbucks to source Fairtrade coffee, and sell it in its outlets, are important in starting to develop this story. The commitment to environmental and social initiatives is interesting but, so far, it is a story inadequately told. 'In Antigua, Starbucks constructed a health and dental clinic for farm workers' is so sketchy that it simply invites cynical questioning. For me it is an opportunity missed to tell an exciting human story in a way that also illustrates some of the deep-seated truths of the brand itself.

For there is also a deeper level of story in Starbucks that links with the sense that this brand, through its shops, creates gathering places for local communities. When people come together in such communities they share stories with each other. In a real sense, the purpose behind Starbucks is to enable the exchange of stories, to help people engage with their own and other people's stories. Go into a Starbucks and I'm sure you'll see what I mean. Have a coffee, listen and observe. People are there in pairs or groups sharing the day's stories of their lives; individuals are reading the day's stories in news-papers or communing with their own thoughts. Starbucks provides the community for such storytelling.

Starbucks has committed more than $750,000 to support six conservation projects in coffee growing regions in Latin America, Asia, and Africa.

**In Panama,** Starbucks provided support to a junior high vocational training school to educate 130 children from some of Panama's poorest families each year.

**In Costa Rica,** Starbucks gave $400,000 to provide books and school supplies for more than 30,000 elementary school students in 382 rural schools.

**In Guatemala,** grants to Enterprise Works Worldwide helped farmers build two coffee processing facilities enabling a cooperative of 700 farm families to improve their economic situation by milling their own coffees.

**In Antigua,** Starbucks constructed a health and dental clinic for farm workers.

**In East Timor,** Starbucks built and equipped a health clinic in an area that had no medical assistance.

our environment

I have started to map out the main routes which I will explore. The nature of a journey is that we seldom travel in a straight line. Language too, which is a central concern of this book, is very rarely at its best when at its most direct. We need time and space to enjoy words. My thesis is that businesses consistently deny time and space to words. In doing so, those businesses become less likeable and they impoverish themselves.

No one wants to be unloved and poor. Brands want to grow and be loved. Growth is the eternal business imperative. To grow you need to make sure all your assets keep working hard for you. Here, in your collective words, is an asset that is present but largely under-nourished in the way we think about brands.

So, let's move on.

**The map of the world** 'We dissect nature along lines laid down by our native language . . . Language is not simply a reporting device for experience but a defining framework for it.' Benjamin Whorf

# The journey before us

If this is a voyage of discovery, what is it we hope to discover? In many ways, as with the great historical voyages, we seek both knowledge and riches. The knowledge we seek is greater understanding of the way brands work through the language they use. The riches might just follow on from that understanding – if brand developers interpret the knowledge well enough and creatively enough to strengthen their emotional links of affection and loyalty with audiences.

To do so, you will need to use words. There's no problem in that, we all use words. The problem has always come simply from a misunderstanding of the real potential of words. As if we once discovered a country of amazing natural resources, which we plundered and squandered then wondered why it was no longer beautiful when we did nothing to renew the resources. We need to care again for the verbal resources we have.

The metaphor reminds us of the way that the European nations 'discovered' and colonized different parts of the world, and in general imposed their cultures and languages as they went. Today we have the legacy in the current map of the world, and the distribution of 'global' languages. The world map can still be shown in different colors, not to portray current empires but linguistic influences. Let's say the pink bits are English-language speaking: USA, UK, Australia, Canada, parts of Africa, Asia, the Caribbean and a pinkish tinge over much of the whole world. Other areas reflect the Spanish and French speakers, following the old trails of colonization. But other languages – including those spoken by the greatest numbers of people – are confined to their own territories, limited by their historical attitudes which meant that they did not seek conquest and expansion.

So there is a global jockeying by languages for power and influence. This needs to be our starting point because, without exploring this, we will lack the maps to go further. We need to understand more of the role played by language in the development of brands, in local and global markets. And the English language is at the center of this exploration. Follow me.

## The global map of language

**Trouble. They are. Words, that is, too much trouble. They come up and hit you in the back of the head. They head off in another direction. Just trouble. More trouble than they're worth. But one word's worth a thousand pictures. Or is it the other way round? They help you find your way around. They take you round in circles. They're a quick way to get from A to B. But still trouble. Words.**

I used those words once for a poster to advertise a talk. I'm always wary about promising too much with words, because they are slippery things. They can be unreliable when you need them in emergency, like those plumbers who advertise '24 hours – 7 days a week' service.

That does not stop me believing in them, though. And when I want to persuade people to do something, naturally I use words and I use words in the language that comes naturally to me. Which happens to be English, because of where and when I was born.

Two thousand years ago my language might well have been Latin. So I find it curious when designers in the 21st century continue to use slabs of Latin text as part of 'design concepts', as if to say: 'Here will go some words. I don't know, perhaps don't care, what those words say. But I do care what they look like.' *Lorem ipsum dolor* gives me grief.

Designers are also saying that they don't want you to be distracted from their design by reading what the words say. So, instead of dog Latin, designers often now use repeated lines saying, 'this is dummy text, it is gibberish and is not intended to have any meaning.' I wonder if that is actually more offensive than the insult to language implied by the use of the nonsense Latin.

But, let's admit it, words can be difficult. They can be elusive, squirming out of your reach just when you thought you had them. We can all be made speechless by things that happen in the world and, in recent years, we seem to have been assaulted by a succession of horrific events. Images of concentration camps, natural disasters and terrorist attacks can move us and strike us dumb. At such times, when journalists themselves struggle for the right words, we feel an even stronger need for words to record, comment and share emotion. Indeed, we have the right to reject the emptiness of clichéd words – 'I saw a scene of indescribable horror' – and demand words that match the emotion of the imagery.

This applies to all kinds of communication, all kinds of emotion – from disgust through to joy, fear to wonder, anger to elation, disappointment to relief. Food packaging needs the same marriage of words and imagery as documentary reportage. It is all about engaging with the thoughts and emotions of others, using verbal and visual means. Typography can be the bridge between the two.

Let's explore some of the possibilities as well as the pitfalls that await us with words. In many ways poetry is the literary form that's closest to design. Read an E E Cummings poem and there seems a clear link to a typographic style that inspired a generation of late-20th-century magazines. The visual arrangement is intriguing, but it is integrated with the meaning of the words.

                                                            (it
was the first ride and believe i we was
happy to see how nice she acted right up to
the last minute coming back down by the Public
Gardens i slammed on
the
internalexpanding
&
externalcontracting
brakes Bothatonce and

brought allof her tremB
-ling
to a :dead

stand –
; still)

Cummings is an extreme example, even considering the typographic look of his own name, but all poets care about the visual appearance of their words. George Herbert in the 17th century wrote poems in the shapes of an altar and a bird in flight to visually reinforce the religious meaning of his verse. Even a form as traditional as, say, the sonnet, has a particular look. If we turn this around, should designers not care as much about the words they are using in their designs as poets do about the designs they are using to express their words?

Of course, many things conspire against this ideal. If poetry is concerned with the choice of precise words, most of our daily life is subjected to the verbal bombardment of mass media. In that world it becomes harder and harder to insist on precision. Our sensibilities are worn down by jargon, slang and code, so what should our attitudes be towards them? We have to avoid rushing to generalized judgments, and be determined to enjoy new forms of language as they come along. Words are there for playing with, but sometimes you laugh with them, and sometimes you laugh at them.

Jargon is nearly always something to laugh at, because you have to suspect its motives. People who use excessive jargon do so to hide their own deficiencies, to confuse others and say 'keep out'. With jargon we have to point out that the emperor has no clothes. Business jargon in particular can leave us floundering but often not wanting to admit it. *You try to pick up on buzzwords, in these coming days of coopetition, while taking a helicopter view of some blue-sky ideas, yet wanting to get into bed with a global partner who offers a strategic fit, in which case you have a win-win situation. But let's talk offline* . . . Bingo!

The main problem with these forms of language is that they provide voluminous cloaks underneath which they hide emaciated thoughts. People can retreat deeper and deeper into poverty-stricken jargon and lose the ability to enjoy the sheer wealth of words. For Wittgenstein 'the limits of my language mean the limits of my world.' There are perhaps a million words in English alone. No one knows how many different languages there are in the world. There is an incalculable number of words used by the human race and those words are changing and evolving constantly. That's something to rejoice in, not to be paralyzed by.

Yet it has been estimated that an educated person's vocabulary amounts to 20,000 words of which only 2,000 might be used in a week. Clearly we all live in tiny linguistic worlds. Imagine what would happen if we could expand them? We might find whole new worlds opening up to us that are currently unseen at the edges of our individual universes.

Yet technology might be driving us in the opposite direction. A recent best-selling book was *wan2tlk? Ltle bk of txt msgs*. Text messaging has brought in its own abbreviated form of language, a special kind of code. Like all codes it aims to be exclusive. Those using it, and understanding it, have the reassurance of communication with like-minded people. But far from being a sign of the imminent death of words, this is another example of the playful potential of language. ITYFIR. I think you'll find I'm right.

Texting is probably not the way you influence people in a business context. At least not yet. It's all about social interaction between generational peers. Slang has always been a way of inventing language to link people together in tribal communities.

Slang can enrich the language, it can bring new words into language and see them disappear again when the times change. There was, for example, a 'lingo' of a time and a social grouping in the Second World War that now seems laughably archaic. But we will probably look back and smile in 20 years' time at the quaintness of some language that is current today.

Perhaps the new word of the new century was 'whassup', a word invented by a brand and by advertising. Budweiser, of course. Because the phrases of advertising tap into the Zeitgeist of a particular moment, they become irritating when the moment has passed. As soon as a politician used the word 'whassup' you knew that the tide had turned against it. But before that happened there was the moment when the Arsenal footballer Thierry Henry scored a goal, ran to the crowd to celebrate, mouthed the word and mimed the gesture

that goes with it. In that moment there was a shared designed experience, uniting the visual and the verbal.

'Whassup' became the word of its time, that time between one century and the next. It was a variant of what has become known as uptalking. Uptalking is something you recognize when it is pointed out to you but it has crept insidiously up on us so that most of the time we do not even recognize its existence. Uptalking is just that way of speech when you add an interrogatory tone to the ends of phrases or sentences. Listen to conversations from *Friends* and perhaps you will slip into it yourself, who knows? It's characterized by 'HRT' (High Rise Terminals), an acronym and a piece of jargon that I like for its irony.

It seems to me that 'whassup' is in this same genre and therefore even more characteristic of its time, reflecting the attitude of not wanting to be seen as absolutely certain of anything. Certainty becomes perceived as arrogance. Arrogance is bad because it represents an adherence to belief. People shy away from that – uptalk is a way of suggesting a belief but simultaneously offering to retract it.

The Microsoft strapline 'Where do you want to go today?' is part of this same trend. So too the line I wrote for Ashridge Business School – 'Do you want to go further?' Straplines, which originated as straightforward statements of functional product benefits – 'Persil washes whiter' – have evolved towards empathetic attempts to engage with the aspirations of a brand's audience.

I saw something of this debate played out at first hand as we began working with Orange. A groundbreaking brand in the UK, Orange had been acquired by France Télécom, and the aim was to spread Orange to markets around the world. But what do you do with one of the brand's prime assets – its strapline 'The future's bright, the future's Orange' – when you export the brand to countries like France, Romania and Cameroon? The word from eastern Europe was that the strapline sounded hopelessly reminiscent of the empty promises of the last days of Communism. Cameroon, a francophone country in Africa, had the same problem as France itself. 'The future's bright, the future's Orange' sounded arrogant; the subtlety of meaning in the English word 'bright' could not be captured in a single French word through translation.

The French plunged ahead with their own advertising, launching Orange in France with the line, 'Le futur, vous l'aimez comment?' This seemed to represent something of a Gallic shrug, rather than the positive, optimistic belief inherent in the English line. France enlisted research and linguistic expert witnesses from la Sorbonne. Here was a philosophical battle between nations and languages, involving points of view about the very nature of life, fought over with words, interpreted through words, but always pointing up the potential for words to have different meanings for different people.

The resolution to the debate lay in the agreement to a single definition of what the Orange brand stood for in all its markets globally. The preferred strapline remained, 'The future's bright, the future's Orange,' but local markets could use straplines in their own languages. These straplines would not be literal translations of the English line but would need to reflect truly the Orange brand essence.

All the world's languages are subject to the influence of other languages. The influences are becoming stronger and stronger as international communication and travel become easier. There is a strong movement towards variants of language with strong regional blends. British English more and more becomes subject to European influence but with a dominant American slant. Australian/New Zealand forms of English will be subject to growing Chinese, Japanese and Asian pressures – and, again, with an American influence. But this trend is not one-way for American English, for that is subject to increasing Hispanic influences, while Miami becomes the world's most powerful Spanish-speaking city in the world's most powerful English-speaking nation.

The point is that a language like English is in a constant state of evolution, and all the stronger for being so. I've been intrigued in recent times by what I call 'Fusion language'. As with Fusion cookery, this is about the mingling of different cultural influences. Fast food is a fast driver of language around the world – from pizza to kebabs, falafel to chop suey, to bagels, balti and Big Macs. Think of all those coffee shops where we now speak the language of cappuccino, espresso and latte to the baristas in this 'third place' between home and work. But Fusion language is rippling out beyond the restaurants and bars. Think of the way car brands communicate with us: 'Spirito di Punto', 'Vorsprung durch Technik', 'Créateur d'automobiles' as the adverts proclaim across Europe and beyond. Implied in all this is the idea that we each have the opportunity to play with words; we have no craving for the familiarity of set ways of saying things. We move on, words move on with us.

In previous times English-speaking cultures used to take in foreign words in an imperialist way. The British, for example, made the Hindi word 'bungalow' into a quintessentially English concept. Now we embrace foreign words in a more cosmopolitan spirit. They add something to our personal brands. We like to associate ourselves with the sophisticated allure of imported words because they can make us feel chic. We don't even need to italicize them to show that they're foreign. They now travel without passports.

CRÉATEUR D'AUTOMOBILES

Spirito
di
Punto

Vorsprung durch Technik www.audi.co.uk Official Fue

Such possibilities open up more with certain kinds of business or product than with others. But the global brands evangelize more confidently without need of a translator. Take, for example, the fashion and cosmetics business, where there has long been a natural affinity with the French language. We all know couturiers, they arrived early in the modern world of English, and eau de cologne had already seen off kölnisch wasser. French adds cachet to scented water. Laboratoires Garnier in English would sound boringly industrial.

But when Tony Soprano in the New Jersey mafia TV series says, 'you mange, Uncle,' inviting him to eat, he displays Italian rather than French roots ('mangiare' not 'manger'). The world's use of American English is largely spread by the broadcast media. In *NYPD Blue* when Sipowicz says, 'We like this guy' we know he means 'We suspect him of committing the crime.' Any of the usual suspects might reply, 'I'm doing good' to the question, 'How ya doin'?' Now if we're a 'do-gooder' the word is spoken with a sneer by the tabloid press. So fundamental words, words like 'good' and 'like', are shifting in meaning through this global language exchange that has been predominantly outwards from America.

Yet, through food and music, American English has been heavily influenced by European tastes and sounds. At the same time the music charts have been frequently invaded by artists singing English which was born in Sweden, Norway, Germany, even Iceland. Of the 24 different nations in the 2002 Eurovision Song Contest only the French managed to sing a song containing no English at all. Fusion English is here, and it deserves to be celebrated because it constantly enriches the base language. There is simply no point in trying to resist and insist on national linguistic purity, because you'll soon be found out for a charlatan. I loved the story of the Australian TV presenter at the Sydney Olympics who refused to speak French (the 'official' Olympic language), saying: 'I know it is traditional but it is also passé.'

If you attempt to stand outside this world of Fusion language, you face the prospect of mounting a futile resistance. The Polish Government has recently tried to repel linguistic incursions, banning the use of foreign words like 'sex shop', 'supermarket', 'music club' and 'plaza'. Attempting to impose Polish language purity, new laws have decreed that 'list elektronczny' should be used instead of 'email'. But, of course, the laws cannot stop emails and the internet smuggling English words into Poland under cover of computers.

It's much more exciting, I believe, to embrace the possibilities of Fusion. There was a lovely moment in an episode of *Frasier* where Niles wanted to go to Seattle's newest Fusion restaurant – a Hawaian / Norwegian version. 'I can't wait to try the coconut herring,' he gushed. For linguistic interest, though, I must just see if Mahi Mahi Smorgasbord is on the menu. Let's tuck in.

But while some words evolve rapidly, others can be fixed in particular periods, and sometimes it's surprising how quickly these contexts and associations can change, leaving the word and its meaning sinking in the wake of time. Times can be defined by a word or phrase that arise from the events or attitudes of that time. For example, it was only in the 1990s that we first heard the phrase 'ethnic cleansing'; now it is evocative of that period but so too are phrases like 'road rage' and 'quality time'. Without being absolutely dated, they give insights into the way we were then and the obsessions that were looming large in many of our lives. Many such words stay without outstaying their welcome, leaving you wondering what word we used before saying, for example, 'teenager' for the first time in the 1940s.

And that is really what is unimaginable. What would we do without words? Even a restriction in our ability to use words leaves us terrified, because words represent our capacity to think and our power to influence. There was much fun made about the US president's way with words when he first came to office in 2001. George W Bush proclaimed that exports mainly come from outside the country, he believed that Nigeria was a major continent and he wanted to bring down the terriers to trade. Language is people, words are their behavior and words can betray meanings that their speakers would like to keep concealed. What 'Dubya's' language betrayed was not his stupidity (don't be fooled) but his prejudices – particularly his xenophobia. In his case, his fear of the 'foreign' easily encompassed those 'snippy' people from the East Coast 'liberal establishment'.

Yet, having lost the election to this man whose linguistic shortcomings they had mocked, what means did the departing White House team use to inflict damage on George W Bush when the new team took over the offices of government? Quite simply, they removed all the W keys from the White House computer keyboards, robbing the incoming administration of its triumphal letter and the symbol of its leader. Strike at your adversary's power. Strike at his ability to use language.

There is an American way with words, just as there is a British, Chinese or Russian way. Home in further and we know that there are regional and local differences in verbal usage. In the end, it comes down to each individual having an idiosyncratic tone of voice which springs from a unique personality. The best design and the best words usually come from a strong sense of individual personality; they come from people putting more of themselves into their work, from not wanting to be seen as being like everybody else.

This means we have to care for words, respecting them for their capacity to do great things. Although language is forever changing, there is a constant core. That core is a wonderful store of words that we can use expressively, in combination with images, to make people laugh or cry, stay or go, sell or buy, make sense of the present or see a vision of the future. We need to think of words as a creative resource not as dummy text.

## The world's language of persuasion

The world is increasingly dominated by business. I say this as objectively as I can, not meaning to imply any political, social or cultural bias. Whether you come from the corporate or the anti-corporate persuasion, or somewhere in the middle, there is almost universal agreement that business (sometimes given an extra emotive twist by the use of the word 'globalization') plays an ever more influential role in our lives.

Business, of course, uses language to communicate. More and more, over the years, it has been using one language to communicate. English. The most widely used language in the world today. So what are we to make of that? Am I expected to throw my hat in the air and shout 'hurrah!' without even wondering whether that is a word that might have emerged from the throats of prehistoric men, a word as universally human as the ability to smile? Native speakers of English are too inclined to make parochial assumptions about the language. I am wary of the triumphalism that accompanies such thinking, and the lazy arrogance that lies behind it.

**Well, if the rest of the world has decided to speak our language, there must be business opportunities for us to exploit. After all, we can't speak any other languages, so we must be removing some significant barriers to our trading performance. For business surely there must be advantages in a single language even more than in a single currency.**

Of course, that comes dangerously close to arrogance. Arrogance in turn leads to complacency. In business terms, complacency generally leads to bankruptcy. So English cannot afford to be complacent about its current role and future place in the world.

But the facts are disarming. Over 85% of international organizations use English as one of their working languages. All the evidence points to English being the most widely used language in the world today. More people are learning English as a second language than speak it as a first language. There is an absolutely mind-boggling number of speakers of Mandarin Chinese in the world. But, they're nearly all in China. And figures also show that more people are learning English in China than speak English as their first language in the rest of the world.

It's easy to see English as the unstoppable juggernaut of languages. It's rolling along toward world domination, but many questions occur, questions that are relevant to a quest to find closer connections between brands and customers. What is this English that these non-English speakers will be speaking? How will that change the language? Who's in control of this? Is the global triumph of English inevitable? And, if so, is that desirable?

The only way for me to try to answer those questions is by first trying to answer these: What lies behind the success of English as a global language? What can we learn from that success?

First, we have to put aside the notion that a language succeeds because it has good rational qualities. For all its attempted logic, Esperanto shows no sign of becoming the global language. English, far from being a simple language, is almost insanely complicated. More than just complicated, but capable of ambiguity that can be wilfully playful or distressingly misleading.

**'How old Cary Grant?' the telegram asked.**
**'Old Cary Grant fine,' came the reply. 'How you?'**

The problem with English is the complexity contained by the simplest words – words such as fine, nice, set. If we take a seemingly simple word like 'set', it takes on different meanings when you see it in a sporting, cooking, social, animal or mathematical context. Context is all, although here we might want to call it a setting.

Clearly English is a language that embraces subtlety and nuance to such an extent that we introduce foreign words like *nuance* when we are seeking *le mot juste*. A stranger to the language must feel set upon by words, in need of a verbal Good Samaritan.

That takes us back to 'set' where we looked briefly before only at the noun. As a verb we change the meaning of 'set' by adding little words to it. So, 'set aside', 'set up', 'set down', 'set in', 'set on', 'set about', all have meanings which leave native speakers bewildered about the core meaning of 'set'.

So, it seems clear to me that the past success and the future prospects of English as a language of business communication do not come from people appreciating the language for its ease of use. In fact, I think the opposite is true. The power of English comes from the playful possibilities opened up by its imprecision and ambiguity. What David Crystal, the linguistic expert, might call its 'ludic' approach. We love giving old words new meanings. We love exploring the different meanings contained in the same word.

Of course it is not only English that has this playful potential. Georges Perec set himself the absurd constraint of writing a novel whose words contained not a single letter 'e'. But the novel was brilliantly translated into English by Gilbert Adair, again without the letter 'e', with the playfully ambiguous title *A void*. It even included a 'translation' of Hamlet's 'To be or not to be' soliloquy as 'Living, or not living'.

Why? you might ask. The writers thought it might be interesting. Like Everest, it was there. More recently the Canadian poet Christian Bök has written a book called *Eunoia*, which means 'beautiful thinking' and happens to be the shortest word in the English language to contain all five vowels. (Let's set aside the fact that the word could not exist in English if it had not been born in Greek.) The point with *Eunoia*, as with Perec, is that the writer creates constraints so that he can try, Houdini-like, to escape them creatively. And I firmly believe that constraints are necessary to achieve real creativity.

But the exercises of Perec and Bök remain exercises. They take the writer and the reader in unusual directions, but in the end they don't really lead anywhere. For example, here is a poem from *Eunoia*, from Chapter O.

**Blond showfolk who do soft porn go to boomtowns to look for work on photo shoots. Molls who hob-nob from mob boss to mob boss croon solos from old torchsongs. Molls who do so do so *molto sordo* too slow for most crowds to follow, so most crowds scoff: *boo, boo*. Folks who do not know how to plot common chords for rock songs or folk songs soon**

**look for good songbooks on how to do so. Folks too
cool to go to sock hops go to Woodstock rock
shows to do pot, bop or doo-wop. Congo bongos
throb to voodoo hoodoo; tom-toms for pow-wows
go *boom, boom*. Gongs go *bong*. Kotos go *bonk*.
Horns honk: *toot, toot*.**

Perhaps not surprisingly, given the limitation of using
'o' as the only vowel, the main meaning emerges from
the sounds that the words make. The writer is almost
driven towards writing about sounds by discovering
that the overuse of one vowel does interesting things to
the sound of his words.

It's all about making choices – and influencing
choice. We all have these choices to make all the time.
What words should I use to influence you? In the
business world, what words will I use to influence you
to buy my product, my brand?

It seems to me that the English-speaking countries
have become particularly focused on the businesses
that make the best use of these skills of building
brands. Brands succeed best when they make a powerful
emotional connection with people who buy them. That
emotional connection needs to be supported by giving
the consumer good rational reasons for the purchase –
basically, 'this product really works.' Other economic
forces at work – the move from manufacturing to
services in the developed industrial world – have accentuated the growth of brands. The 'new industries' are
knowledge, communication, entertainment. Learning,
information, leisure. Industries with foreseeably good
growth prospects.

More than that though, these are industries where
English-speaking countries have real expertise – and
which use the English language as an essential element
of their way of doing business. To the extent that

business itself will continue to be the principal influence on the way the world develops, English has to be seen as being in a vital strategic position.

Of course, unforeseeable political or environmental developments could still change all that. But business is good at coping with threats and challenges – and adapting to meet those challenges. Even recent history demonstrates that.

Perhaps the main threat is an internal one. By this, I mean the possibility of a reaction against everything that people see business as standing for. This could be a crisis of confidence in brands triggered by attacks on, say, Coca-Cola and McDonald's. Global brands have come under attack, and there is no doubt that many of these brands have not been admirable in their business behavior. The debate has been healthy. It has brought about some change, and more is needed.

But, unlike Naomi Klein, I do not believe that every big brand has a malevolent purpose. There is no doubt, though, that there is a moral challenge facing all brands. How can brands, how can businesses, change the world for the better? How can they develop a stronger ethical sense? If these are the demands that consumers make of brands, then brands will change to meet those demands – or they will become unloved and reviled and will go into decline.

In other words, brands rise and fall constantly. There is nothing inevitable in the continuing rise of a brand. Increasingly we see that language plays a key role in the development and adaptability of a brand. Without this willingness to adapt, a brand may well not survive.

The McDonald's example is interesting. In my previous book, *We, me, them & it*, I referred to some businesses using the linguistic equivalent of junk food. McDonald's has never been the world's worst offender in this, although it does employ a very restricted vocabulary. That very restriction, and the simplicity and populism that go with it, might be one factor behind the company's worldwide growth. At the same time, it has made the brand easy to identify as a 'villain' in a world where Generation X is frustrated by a diet of McJobs.

McDonald's has spread its McLanguage to every major town in the world. It has even legally registered over 100 phrases as its own. Phrases like: 'Good Jobs for Good People', 'Have You Had Your Break Today?' and 'Hey, It Could Happen' as well as the more expected Big Mac and Filet-o-Fish.

Along the way, as it has blazed its trail to non-English-speaking countries, it has made small concessions to other languages. In *Pulp Fiction* there is a bizarre conversation about McDonald's between the characters played by John Travolta and Samuel L Jackson. It's a great bit of writing that shows how language is a crucial part of the McDonald's identity that is recognized worldwide – and a demonstration that recognition is more valuable than registration.

> Vincent **In Paris, you can buy beer at McDonald's. Also, you know what they call a Quarter Pounder with Cheese in Paris?**
>
> Jules **They don't call it a Quarter Pounder with Cheese?**
>
> Vincent **No, they got the metric system there, they wouldn't know what the fuck a Quarter Pound is.**
>
> Jules **What'd they call it?**
>
> Vincent **Royale with Cheese.**
>
> Jules (repeating) **Royale with Cheese. What'd they call a Big Mac?**
>
> Vincent **Big Mac's a Big Mac, but they call it Le Big Mac.**

Ronald McDonald became Donald McDonald in Japan because of the lisping difficulties of Japanese tongues with the letter 'R'. There have been minor cultural concessions too. In India the Maharaja Mac is a vegetarian burger because beef and pork burgers cannot be countenanced. McDonald's itself insists that it is not a global company, but a local company operating independently in each of its markets.

Most of us will be skeptical about that. Experience seems to tell us otherwise. Yet it is a fact that in France there was a McDonald's advertising campaign that poked fun at America and American eating habits. The abiding impression, though, remains that of an American company whose brand throughout the world contains a large element of Americanness. That is what people have seen as its attraction.

The trouble for McDonald's is that there is evidence that people might not continue to do so as enthusiastically as they have in the past. The 'can do' spirit of America still appeals, but there are aspects of America that are less popular worldwide and McDonald's is closely associated with these: over-indulgence, quantity before quality, speed at the expense of relaxation, eating for comfort rather than need.

Of course, a lot of smaller companies will also be damned with such criticisms, but McDonald's is there (everywhere) and it is big. And for McDonald's one of its biggest problems is that it does not have the flexibility of language to mount a convincing enough response when its core business is under this kind of threat. The grail remains invisible for now. So, part of its strategy is to stretch its brand into new areas, such as hotels, and at the same time to acquire new brands that are not tainted with the same issues. Will this strategy succeed? Only, I believe, if McDonald's really allows these brands to develop in their own independent ways.

Pret-a-Manger is a case in point, a brand that developed in opposition to many of the McDonald's principles. Now that it has been part-acquired by McDonald's, will it be allowed to stick to the principles that made it strong? Interestingly, Pret-a-Manger is an example, even in its name, of the development of fusion language. This brand's approach to language is part of its commitment to quality, to being 'passionate about food'. There is a distance for McDonald's to travel if it is to understand the brand and not stifle it. Understanding the brand means understanding the potential for subtlety and adaptability in language and culture.

Let me illustrate this by staying in this accessible territory of food. After all, we all eat. We probably all eat in restaurants or cafés sometimes. I came across these three examples of restaurants using words in different ways to recruit staff. From each example you will get a clear sense of what the brand is aiming to convey.

This first one is actually from a perfectly good café near where I live in London. One Saturday morning I walked in and saw these words taped to the door: 'Experienced Breakfast Chef Wanted'. The notice was hand-written, you could almost see the behind-the-scenes desperation. After that I wasn't sure about the breakfast I ate – but I gave the brand another chance because I knew it well. (By the way, just down the road was a clothes retailer that was advertising for 'Sales consultants wanted. No experience necessary.')

The second restaurant example was from near where I work, just off the Strand in London. They placed this sign in the window: 'Charming, intelligent waiting staff – one more wanted.' I would say that this example engages – it conveys a likeable personality. Which I suggest is the challenge for English in the future, indeed the challenge for all languages. But does

Charming, intelligent waiting staff — one more wanted.

**passion** & pride, **careers** & reward, heart & soul

We are opening new Prets, one at a time, no rush.
We need to employ more wonderful people.
And we visit www.pret.com
0800 783 7883 or visit www.pret.com

English have a greater ability to make that kind of engagement than other languages?

There's a danger of generalization, so let me give you a third example to develop the point further. Neither of the first two examples were 'brands' in any large-scale sense, but here is Pret-a-Manger, a brand now strong in the UK and starting to spread in the USA. This is the napkin Pret-a-Manger recently offered you when you bought a sandwich from them. They took the unusual step of using the napkins as a recruitment ad. I think it gives you a good feeling about the company – and it almost certainly makes both potential and existing staff feel positive towards the brand.

As I said before, it's all about choices.

I have deliberately used recruitment advertising to illustrate my point and move the argument onto people – the people who work for companies and brands. Brands are represented by people. There is simply no point trying to project a brand with clearly defined values if the brand representatives then undermine or contradict those values. This will become an increasingly important issue for all brands. The internal development of a brand, ensuring that its values are truly understood and lived by its people, is essential to ensure consistent external communication. But we need to be very careful that we do not try to turn people into robotic representatives, all wearing the same uniform, the same smile and speaking the same words.

Earlier I made the point about the need for business to be playful with words, a playfulness that English has always possessed. Again, it seems to me that the developing business climate is, for this reason in particular, favoring English.

In *We, me, them & it*, I wrote about the need to create a brand's tone of voice by achieving a balance between the demands of the company itself, the individual, and the audiences we address. My plea was, 'Bring more of your own personality to work and put it in your own writing.'

That remains an essential component of creative business writing. And I believe most business writing should be creative. Here is a diagram that recognizes, however, that there are different levels of business writing. Perhaps we achieve the top level of this diagram rarely. We need to achieve it more often.

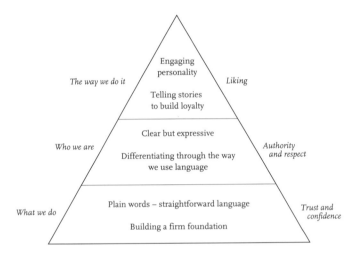

The triangle here has a foundation, a central section and a peak. Each segment represents a different form of writing that a company might use.

The foundation level is about using language to establish trust and confidence. We might describe this as 'plain words' – using simple, clear, direct language, avoiding ambiguity and jargon. But this kind of language simply establishes the generic values that any business might be expected to have – a basic level of efficiency and clarity.

Plain words, though, take you only so far. If every brand simply used plain words, there would be no differentiation and no interest in the communication. So, in the next level, a brand can use language which establishes its authority and builds respect, as well as a sense of the brand's personality. Some of the language used at this second level will be language that is specific to the kind of industry in which the company operates.

Added to that, at the top level, here is an approach to language that is much more expressive. Here we encourage the brand to have fun with language. If so, the brand will build a liking as well as respect and trust, and will make clear what is really different about this brand. The brand can tell stories; it can use different forms and different kinds of language. The most differentiated brands will combine all three levels of this triangle.

I believe that this suggests another reason why English will continue to grow as a global language. It is simply a virtuous circle. English works well with global brands. Global brands work well with English. There is a mutually reinforcing growth cycle.

But I must guard against any whiff of triumphalism for the English language because, as I have already said, I believe that breeds the attitude that could then destroy English's place in the world. Earlier I asked two questions, and now that I have given them a context, I will answer them.

### Is the 'global triumph of English' inevitable? And, if so, is that entirely desirable?

I would answer 'no' to both questions. The biggest threat to the ability of English-speaking business to exploit the advantages of English-speaking is, paradoxically, the chronic inability of English mother-tongue speakers to perform in other languages. Because hand in hand with that failure goes the inability to understand other cultures. Businesses will not succeed if they are unable to build understanding of others – particularly, of course, customers.

As this century advances, English will become less and less shaped by the cultures of English-speaking nations. English will become the second language of more and more people. Business situations will increasingly arise where the meeting is conducted in English, but the majority of participants will be speakers of English as a second language. Who will understand each other better in these situations? That will be the challenge for the native English speaker – to understand and not to assume that superior knowledge of English confers a benefit of understanding. The amazing growth among UK companies of call centers based in India is an interesting development – particularly when you read that the Indian telephone operators, all graduates, are trained in British culture, not just English language. This means having to watch the latest episode of a soap opera like the London-based *EastEnders*, knowing the weekend's football results and being prompted to talk about the weather on their computer screens by up-to-the-minute reports of sun, snow or rain affecting the British Isles.

English in 2050 will be very different from that spoken today – just as 50-year-old newsreels seen today show how far the language has evolved in our life span. With technological changes – digital broadcasting, texting on mobile phones, the growth of emails as well as the internet – English is going through a period of accelerating evolution, with English mingling more and more with cultural influences from different parts of the world. This has always been a feature of English. The import–export trade of words into the English

language and into other languages is a healthy one. People can even trade jokes across linguistic boundaries now, as I saw from the name of this Parisian patisserie-cum-sandwich shop – 'Plaisirs et Pains'.

Just as I welcome that, I also worry about the threat to what we might call linguistic biodiversity. Will the world, as predicted by the founders of the Rosetta project, lose 50% of its languages over the next 100 years? I think the English language, and all languages, are impoverished by such losses.

There is a very fluid situation with languages today. Fluidity is encouraged by economic growth, by increasing travel, by the internet. In this situation there are short-term opportunities for English-speaking countries to use their English language fluency to gain business advantage. English is, in effect, an invisible export within most of the products, and certainly the services, these countries sell. But they cannot assume that their 'mastery' of current English will give them a continuing advantage in the future business world.

They have to think of the longer term and they have to develop a change of attitude toward English and other languages. We see two seemingly conflicting trends at work. First, the poor skills native English speakers have in learning languages and cultures other than their own. Secondly, the amazing adaptability of the language itself.

In other words, English will change rapidly even if native English speakers do not.

If English speakers are to exploit this current language advantage, the paradox is that they need to become better at understanding other languages and cultures. They have to see English itself (in all its forms) as a new language to learn – and keep learning.

As part of this necessary flexibility, there is a need to loosen our approach to the use of English in business.

We need to use words as we speak them, and stop hiding behind the barriers of professional jargon and outdated stuffiness that keep businesses remote from their audiences. We must allow individuals to express their individuality at work through less bureaucratic, less corporate language. All businesses are becoming brands, and brands will need to embrace both consistency and diversity – a difficult trick, but an essential one. The boringly uniform will fade away. The survivors will use more expressive, diverse forms of English.

There are enormous challenges and opportunities for English-speaking businesses here. Businesses have to use language to communicate – to use English in all its coming forms. Through language they need to engage with customers and potential customers. That takes language and communication skills. Will companies have those skills? They will if they rise above the level of Plain Words and welcome the idea of truly expressive English in business communication.

One final point. No one should take a 'little Englander' attitude to English. See it as a young baby and not an old man. Approach the future with an attitude of being ready to learn rather than ready to teach. Earlier, I said that there is nothing inevitable in the continuing rise of any brand. You have to look after brands by giving them space and creativity in order to encourage development. In many ways, English is a brand too, and it's a global one. All users of English have to look after English, not by stifling and stunting it with misplaced kindness, but by giving it some freedom. Then it will become richer than ever and deserve to be the global language, because it will not only influence but be influenced by the other languages of the world.

Just as I finished reading the proofs of this chapter, Alastair Creamer from Unilever rang me to point out an interview in the *Guardian* with the travel writer, Robyn Davidson.

> **Travel is only useful if you go open to the possibility of surrendering parts of what had formed you in exchange for the new perspectives offered by difference – if you go out of curiosity and respect. If you enter a place *on its own terms*. But tourism is travel with its heart ripped out.**

That seemed to me to strike the right note. When it comes to language, and the development of English in particular, we all need to become travelers not tourists, curious and respectful, open to the possibilities of different views and different pathways. So, let's see what is happening with some people already traveling.

**Those already traveling** '*The two most engaging powers of an author are to make new things familiar and familiar things new.*'
Samuel Johnson

# Engaged on the journey

In the previous chapter we embarked on our quest to find the grail which enables brands to form stronger emotional ties with their audiences. Is the grail to do with language itself? Is it, more particularly, to do with the English language? The answers point to 'yes' but there are still questions and there is more to discover. Is the grail about creating connections between the brand and its customers? Is it about creating better conversations and relationships with customers as a result?

As we move forward, sketched map in hand, one word seems to resound like a bell rung by a guide who points our way. The word is 'engaging'. I had thought it a particularly contemporary word until I came across the Samuel Johnson quotation that introduces this chapter. Even in the 18th century Johnson was speaking of an author's 'engaging powers'.

While working with the National Theatre recently I had described its need to be intellectually, emotionally and socially engaging. The National Theatre, as the UK's (and world's) standard-bearer for the theatre, cannot 'dumb down'. Our intellect needs to be satisfied by the thoughts and ideas raised by theatre, while our emotions are brought into play by the immediacy of live performance. At the same time, theatre has to prove its continuing relevance and show that it can welcome and speak to all sections of society.

Naturally, this being theatre, there was no need to argue for the power of words. Yet, even here, there was too easy an acceptance that great words are performed only on stage. 'Front of house' rarely indulged in much more than a polite, deferential mumble – which makes it hard to engage with audiences and create a dramatic experience outside as well as inside the auditoria.

A friend of mine, Will Awdry, who's a creative director in advertising, showed me a copy of a document he had written for his company. It was called *Engagement – a tract*. The *engaging* word seemed to be pursuing me. Prompted by Will's thinking, I offered him my own definition: 'Engaging communication is about inviting yourself memorably into other people's minds.' This definition seemed to fit well with Will's own words, such as: 'For a nation of shopkeepers, we're not very good at selling. We're actually much better at making people want to buy. Economic culture in the UK is about seduction not rape.'

Actually I'm not sure that these implied differences in ways of marketing are simply a sign of a cultural divide between the UK and the USA. I believe there is also, and perhaps more importantly, a separation between the old and the new. The mega US brands, which grew big in days of unsophisticated competition, were good at selling. The newer US brands, not yet mega, are growing because they are good at making people want to buy. Crate and Barrel, Motley Fool, Amazon, for examples. All economic culture now needs to be about seduction. But there are still many different ways to seduce and be seduced.

It seems to me that these brands succeed because they engage their customers in more interesting conversations than the more traditional brands. Of course, you need interesting words to have interesting conversations. A quirky yet very American brand that takes this approach is McSweeney's, who offer books and magazines of a particularly idiosyncratic kind. But McSweeney's is less a book club than a network of like-minded individuals. It hardly seems to be a business at all, so well does it shelter behind an ironic veil of amateurism, yet McSweeney's has a powerful following among the people who make up its natural audience.

These are people who love words and stories: and the man behind McSweeney's, the man writing the words, is Dave Eggars, author of *A heartbreaking work of staggering genius*. Something interesting is happening here. A literary writer creates not just an international best-selling book but also a business that is developing into a distinctive brand. Its words are what make it distinctive.

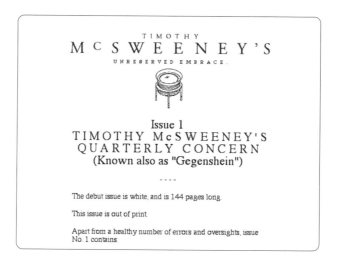

TIMOTHY
M ᶜ S W E E N E Y ' S
UNRESERVED EMBRACE.

Issue 1
TIMOTHY McSWEENEY'S
QUARTERLY CONCERN
(Known also as "Gegenshein")

- - - -

The debut issue is white, and is 144 pages long.

This issue is out of print.

Apart from a healthy number of errors and oversights, issue No. 1 contains:

Our times have changed. The whole context in which business operates now is different from that of the last century. Consumers are much more elusive – they don't just play hard to get, they are hard to get. Skepticism is rife, particularly among younger consumers. There are more influences brought to bear on all of us, we are all surrounded by distractions, encouraging us toward shorter attention spans. We live more complicated lives; it becomes harder to predict what we will be doing, what we will be like, in the near future. There are no mass groupings of people under broad consumer categories of A,B,C1/C2. Who now buys the soap powder? Is it a white housewife with two children? If so, we'll have to find a different way to describe her and to understand her lifestyle. Because society itself has evolved into a state of diversity that can no longer be described by the old categorizations of classical marketing. How should we make sense of this diversity without complicating things to an absurd extent?

**A brand is a storehouse of trust. That matters more and more as choices multiply. People want to simplify their lives.**
Niall FitzGerald, Unilever

This does not mean that people now want simple brands. They want brands that will make their lives simpler, which means that brands have to work harder to deliver that service to customers. We ask more of brands now than the reassurance of 'Trust me, I'm big.' We ask brands to deliver great service, which includes the requirement to *entertain* the customer. Brands can make us laugh. And they use words to do so. Yet conventional marketing wisdom has long held that humor is too risky an element to use at the heart of a brand.

Actually, with words you cannot avoid humor, so why try? The appointment of Douglas Daft as the chairman of Coca-Cola seemed to send a signal that humor can never be suppressed in modern commercial life. Brands need more jokes. Later in this chapter I will explain in more detail some examples such as the international toiletries group Lush. Go into any Lush shop, as I first did a couple of years ago, and your senses are attacked by color and fragrance and also by a wealth of sparky words. On that first visit I bought some talcum powder simply because it made me smile. It was called *Dust to Dust* and underneath the name it said: '*Can you hear me, Aunty Joy?' You'll always come up smelling of roses.*

Think too of a brand like Ben & Jerry's. *Cherry Garcia* (named when the Grateful Dead's Jerry Garcia died) strikes me as the best bad-taste (but respectful) joke yet to find its way onto packaging. For Caramel Chew-chew ice cream they begin: '*Caramel lovers rejoice!*' I don't like caramel but I might just reconsider, particularly when they go on: '*Admittedly we're biased . . .*'

Words send signals, whether we want them to or not – signals about who we are and what we are really like. We should make sure we are sending the right signals. Companies and brands send signals through their words. They need to care about the signals they send, but too often they ignore them completely. Brands, like US presidents, like all of us, can easily 'mis-speak'.

The fact is that people are now watching to see if Ben & Jerry's starts to mis-speak. The reason for the watchfulness is that Ben & Jerry's was acquired by Unilever. Unilever bought Ben & Jerry's because it had a strong brand. In financial terms it was not particularly significant for a company of Unilever's size. At about the same time that it was buying Ben & Jerry's for $326 million, Unilever bought Bestfoods for $20 billion. Whereas Bestfoods was seen as a straightforward corporate acquisition, much like any other, the purchase of Ben & Jerry's was seen by many (on the Ben & Jerry's side) as a sell-out. Those who loved Ben & Jerry's loved more than just the products; they admired its social and environmental commitments, they enjoyed the humor of its product names and descriptions, they liked the personalities of the two founders.

So how will a business built as 'anti-corporate' make the transition into the corporate world? Will it remain true to its principles and its brand values?

Time will tell, but interesting stories began to emerge after Yves Couette was appointed by Unilever as chief executive. Is the spirit of Ben & Jerry's indomitable? Asked by the new chief executive to produce a 'brand key', the staff decided to go about it in a Ben & Jerry's way rather than a Unilever way. So they renamed it a brand cone and came up with the motto '*Joy to the belly and soul.*'

The early signs, therefore, were that Ben & Jerry's might change Unilever more than Unilever would change it. Unilever has now published a social audit and has continued donating a proportion of profits to charities. But the change of ownership changed perceptions to the extent that Ben & Jerry's dropped from No. 5 to No. 30 in *The Wall Street Journal*'s list of socially responsible firms.

Yves Couette understands that he needs to manage this transition with care. 'Ben was saying the other day that business is a powerful force. If businesses decided to do something, they could change the world. The impact on the world is enormous.' Will Unilever have more influence to change the world than Ben & Jerry's in its independent days? Will it have the words to do so? Or will it not understand how to use the distinctive language created by the Ben & Jerry's brand that sprang out of a belief in social justice, environmental responsibility and respect for local communities? As well as a great sense of humor.

We will see. It is too early to say now. But Unilever is a company that understands brands well, and there is no reason to expect the worst.

In this chapter we are looking at brands that have developed by placing particular emphasis on their language and in particular on projecting externally to their customers the internal ethos and beliefs of the company. They use engaging words to do so, words that build a bridge between the philosophy of the people who originally created the brand and those people outside the company who are attracted to that philosophy.

My belief is that brands are differentiated by their visual and verbal identity. The visual identity of a brand is made up of familiar elements such as a logotype, symbol, typeface and colors. But we're less used to thinking of a brand's verbal identity, which might include its name, strapline, stories and tone of voice. In short, its words.

Let us explore this through some particular examples. Innocent, Lush, Egg. By definition, because these are brands that have grown in response to a changed business environment and a different attitude to marketing in that environment, these are not major multinational brands. They have not yet had time to reach that kind of scale, and perhaps it is not even in the business philosophies of these companies to aim for that. But we now live in a world where even the most ubiquitous of global brands insist that they are small and local at heart. We'll think about that one. My point is simply that all brands, big or small, mature or developing, are in competition to win our trust, respect and liking. The words that they use are the key to achieving that aim.

## An innocent tale

I was first introduced to Innocent smoothies when Simon White from Lever Fabergé came along to one of my workshops clutching four bottles. I had asked all the participants to bring with them an example of business writing that they liked. People came with leaflets, booklets, carrier bags, training manuals. And Simon brought three bottles of smoothies and one thickie.

Innocent arouse that kind of messianic enthusiasm in people. Simon could have bought a single bottle but he wanted to show the range and variety of the products and the words that they used. 'Listen,' he said, reading the label of the cranberries and raspberries smoothie.

**My mum's started buying our smoothies (and that's after a whole year, the skinflint).**

**I've got to behave and not say anything too rude or controversial. So, mum, they are really good for you. They are made with 100% pure fresh fruit. They contain loads of vitamin C (a day and a half's worth). They are as fat free as an apple or banana, and that's because they are just fruit. Is that good enough for you, mum?**

**Right, I'm off to smash some windows and have a fag.**

Everyone enjoyed Simon reading that label out loud, so we got him to read two more. They were just as funny, but still making serious points about the fact that these smoothies are made of fruit and nothing but fruit – and they're good for your health. Somehow I believed these words more than a straightforward statement with the same message. Or was it simply that I really took in the message because I had been fully engaged by it?

The enjoyment in the words went beyond these passages of description. When you looked on the label and the bottle every detail of wording had been thought about. On the bottle top there was an 'enjoy by' date, not a 'use by' or 'sell by'. Then there was playfulness around the legal marks – for example © = chicken free, ® = really really nice, ™ = tasty mixtures. The ingredients were listed exactly but you might find the odd surprise:

**2 pressed apples**
**1/2 mashed banana**
**11 crushed raspberries**

**Ingredients (minimum contents)**
2½ pressed apples,
6 crushed strawberries,
½ mashed banana,
a dash of freshly squeezed orange juice
and a few small pebbles*.

**Nutritional Information (per 100ml)**
Energy 196Kj (47 Kcal)
Protein 0.4 g
Carbohydrates 10.7 g
 of which sugars 10.3 g
Fat 0.2 g
Fibre 0.6 g
Sodium 7 mg
Vitamin C 38 mg
Innocent 100 %

This bottle provides
150% RDA of natural Vitamin C

*we lied about the pebbles

le
day.

5 038862 320108

**50 crushed cranberries**
**a dash of freshly squeezed orange juice**
**and 1 small church***

**\*not really**

The labels were simple two-color printing, with the words in black type and the cheery little logo in color – a fruit with the suggestion of a face and a halo. Purely innocent. As well as smoothies there were fresh yogurt thickies, which had puzzles on the labels, to sit and figure out while you had your breakfast. And following on from the ingredients the words *'separation can sometimes occur\*'* with the asterisk being answered lower down the label with *'\*but mummy still loves daddy.'*

Following this introduction at the workshop, I started looking out for Innocent drinks. They were not that difficult to find. The coffee shops seemed to be stocking them, then shortly after some big supermarkets like Sainsbury's and Waitrose. I started buying and drinking the product – and really liking it. I noticed too that the labels were constantly changing. It reminded me of childhood days when I used to read the cereal packets and sauce bottles – but this was better because the words were always different.

I decided to find out more. There was a great website which told the story of how the whole company began.

In the summer of 1998 when we had developed our first smoothie recipes but were still nervous about giving up our proper jobs, we bought £500 worth of fruit, turned it into smoothies and sold them from a stall at a little music festival in London. We put up a big sign saying 'Do you think we should give up our jobs to make these smoothies?' and put out a bin saying 'YES' and a bin saying 'NO' and asked people to put the empty bottle in the right bin. At the end of the weekend the 'YES' bin was full so we went in the next day and resigned.

That's a terrific story. It's an example of the way companies can use storytelling techniques to build their brands. In this case it was about creating a legend, a legend that is totally believable and completely in the spirit of the brand that has since been carried through consistently. The story expresses a fundamental truth about the character of the company.

On another part of the site there were the inevitable FAQs – not normally my favorite section of a website. But there were some unusual differences here.

*Where are your drinks made?*

Our juices are made out in the country. The fruit gets squeezed and bottled overnight and arrives in your town early in the morning. We check the juices and send them out in our little chiller vans around town, getting them to you as fast as our little wheels will carry us.

*Where did I put my keys?*

They're behind your commemorative Wedgwood Queen Mother ornament.

Of course, that's right. 'Where did I put my keys?' is a frequently asked question in any house, in any country. Like the occasional fake addition to the ingredients list, the FAQs are lightened by the odd daft question – 'How are babies made?' 'Do you think I should dye my hair?' The technique keeps you reading, keeps you intrigued, and helps you to absorb the majority of the information that is purely factual but lightly told in answer to questions like 'Where do you get your fruit?' 'Can children drink your products?' 'How long do they last?' The overall message is that these are natural products – 'made by nature'.

**If you've enjoyed your smoothie, why not try our other products like sand, rainbows, or perhaps plankton?**

Everywhere the message was repeated insistently and, it seemed, genuinely, that Innocent Drinks was enjoying the conversation and hoped you were too. 'Why not say hello?' it said on the label. Why not indeed? So I got in touch with Innocent Drinks and arranged to meet Richard Reed.

It was just a short journey. I didn't think Innocent would be far, and there they were just a few stops along the tube line. I made for Innocent's office at Shepherd's Bush.

Fruit Towers is, of course, a single-level industrial shed on the Goldhawk Trading Estate. Naturally it's not grand, this is a young company with a small staff and a big sense of humor. Fruit Towers is in *Minder* territory, the TV series featuring dodgy deals and characters in West London. This is the kind of place where the lead dodgy character, Arthur Daley, would have had one of his more legitimate lock-ups. But don't be fooled by appearances, trust your experience. Behind the seedy exterior, everything is innocent.

If you've enjoyed your smoothie, why not try our other products like sand, rainbows, or perhaps plankton.

Made by nature

Richard Reed is one of three founders of Innocent Drinks. They've been going only since 1998, having met originally at university, scattered to do jobs in various kinds of consultancy, but stayed friends. Each time they met for a drink, they talked about setting up a business together. Then, in 1998, they decided that the time was right to put their money where their mouths were.

'So the story is true then?' I asked. Indeed it was, Richard told me. He, Adam and Jon kept meeting and moaning about their jobs (in advertising and management consultancy) and they realized that their lifestyles were completely unhealthy. Their working lives meant long days and snatched meals. Their last healthy meal was probably when they each went home for Sunday lunch at their parents' houses. So that led to the thought that they ought to make a natural, fresh food/drink product. They all know the theory about healthy nutrition but they, like most people, had done nothing to achieve it in their personal lives. 'So rather than preach, we should just get on and deliver it. We asked lots of people and everyone said we should use concentrates, flavorings, preservatives if we were going to make fruit drinks. We decided we should be about one thing, and only one thing. You might call that Nature.'

The £500 worth of fruit was bought and the smoothies were sold. Highflying jobs were resigned. All around them health scares were breaking out daily in the newspapers, giving them increased conviction in the rightness of their proposition that it does not make sense to mess about with Nature. Even though their actions seem shot through with innocence, the original brand name was Fast Tractor. Yet, although the visual presentation of the Fast Tractor brand was completely different, the verbal style was the Innocent style right from the start. The verbal style springs from a deeply felt but lightly worn belief in what they are doing –

carried off by the force of their own personalities. They stress first the importance of honesty and integrity, which gives them the inner belief to trust in the intelligence of their customers.

I asked Richard if they had ever had complaints about the listing of ingredients such as 'two plump nuns' or 'three traffic cones' alongside bananas, mangoes and raspberries. Apparently the Trading Standards officers had asked questions but had acted with common sense. Lawyers can smile too. The ® mark is legally registered, but who says it can't stand for 'really really nice'?

The original idea was to keep the labels as fresh as the product, which meant producing new labels daily. That was impossible to sustain, but there are still new labels every week. Richard has now passed on the baton, and most of the writing is done by Dan Germain. Printing costs of two-color labels are cheap, and they know that customers read the labels like newspapers, so it's important to keep changing them. Every Thursday at 5 o'clock there is a meeting of the Bad Joke Committee and they thrash out ideas for what should appear on future labels. The determination not to contribute to 'homogenization of the planet' extends beyond the product to the brand.

Always though, the messages are consistent about Innocent's core principles. The central one is that nature is best, but there is a little book of company rules. The company rulebook is available to customers because Rule 2 is: *'Always ask an expert. What's the answer? We don't know. Most of the time we don't even know the question. But there's always someone we can turn to. And that's you, dear reader. We couldn't have done it without you.'* If you want to get in touch, to have a chat or some ideas, you are asked to email them on iamabit-bored@innocentdrinks.co.uk, which is just a final example of the way this brand has a consistent verbal identity running through everything it does.

As I leave, Richard offers me a lift into town in half an hour in one of the Innocent vans. I thank him but I have to get back, so I head for the tube. Outside Fruit Towers a van is parked. It has the Innocent logo, and is painted in black and white to look like a cow. There are eyelashes over the headlamps and horns on each wing. I regret passing up the chance to drive through Central London in the cow van. Instead I sit on the tube and write my version of an Innocent label which I will email to Richard to say thank you. It goes like this:

**It must have been one of those kids' parties when I was little. Was it Jimmy Beecham's birthday? Anyway a man turned up with a big, black, pointy hat with silver stars stuck on it, waved a wand and said 'abracadabra'. Memory plays tricks too. I think that was when I had my first drink made with real fruit and nothing else. Since then I keep doing it. Never fails.**

**™ = totally magical**

**A life that's Lush**

Lush makes fresh handmade cosmetics and sells them in the UK, Australia, Brazil, Canada, Croatia, Denmark, Holland, Italy, Japan, and many other letters of the alphabet.

Lush is a brand which appeals first to your sense of smell, then to your sense of color, and then to your sense of humor. It happens in that order as you approach a shop and then go inside. In many ways it's quite mad. Products are given daft names as if to challenge you to believe in them despite everything your reason might tell you. 'Buffy the Backside Slayer' is a body conditioner that's 'full of natural exfoliants and skin softening butters to fight cellulite and smooth bumpy bits'. The name suggests that this is all a bit of a laugh. This is quite a different approach from the shop across the way that might say 'Exfoliant soap scrub' on the grounds that 'we understand that this is a serious subject and we recognize that you work hard at keeping yourself looking good.'

It can be important to be earnest but, when you think about it, this is a very funny subject. We all like to look good but we all know that beauty is in the eye on the beholder. Most of us reach the stage, long before we want to, when we spend more time looking at ourselves in mirrors than other people spend looking at us. And we know that there's no fooling ourselves. We grow old, we grow old, and our self-image gets unrolled before our eyes. The only thing to do is laugh. That, at least, is the honest reaction which lingers just beneath the skin in most of us.

Lush taps into that, both the humor and the honesty. The Lush approach to language is driven primarily by its approach to product development. Both are founded on honesty. When you've bought your new stuff for smooth bumpy bits or rough flaky bits, the assistant pops it in a bag. The bag proclaims:

**A LUSH LIFE**
**WE BELIEVE**

**... in making effective products out of fresh organic\* fruit and vegetables, the finest essential oils and safe synthetics, without animal ingredients, and in writing the quantitative list on the outside.**

**We also believe in buying only from companies that test for safety without the involvement of animals and in testing our products on humans.**

**We believe in making our own fresh\* products by hand, printing our own labels and making our own fragrances.**

**We believe in long candlelit baths, massage, filling the house with perfume and in the right to make mistakes, lose everything and start again.**

**We believe that our products should be good value, that we make a profit and that the customer is always right.**

**\*We also believe words like 'fresh' and 'organic' have honest meaning beyond marketing.**

Now there's something. Here is a company that points out that words are often misused in the commercial game that's played between seller and consumer. Words can be used to deceive. In particular, words like

# A LUSH LIFE
## WE BELIEVE

...in making effective products out of fresh organic* fruit and vegetables, the finest essential oils and safe synthetics, without animal ingredients, and in writing the quantitative list on the outside.

We also believe in buying only from companies that test for safety without the involvement of animals and in testing our products on humans.

We believe in making our own fresh* products by hand, printing our own labels and making our own fragrances.

We believe in long candlelit baths, massage, filling the house with perfume and in the right to make mistakes, lose everything and start again.

We believe that our products should be good value, that we make a profit and that the customer is always right.

*We also believe words like "fresh" and "organic" have honest meaning beyond marketing 'fresh' and 'organic' have honest meaning only if they are used precisely. Lush's claim, therefore, is that it uses words precisely to describe its products with absolute honesty.

It's a big claim. Can we believe it? I asked Sarah McCartney who has for some years written most of the words for Lush. (When you think about it, this is the opposite approach to Gerald Ratner who thought he was being honest and funny when he said, a few years ago in the UK, that most of the jewelry sold in his eponymous shops was 'crap'. The honesty was out of place because it never extended to the way the products were actually sold as 'great value'. End of Gerald Ratner and of the Ratners brand. I mention the Ratners example because it proves how difficult an area this is. If you laugh at, not with, your customers, you are lost.)

Sarah McCartney walks in and starts talking. There is something about her that tells you quickly that she is the personification of the Lush brand. Lush makes a product called 'Ballistic' – a ball that contains sodium bicarbonate which then fizzes as the natural ingredients and fragrances dissolve in the hot running water of a bath. Sarah drops Ballistic-like into a conversation.

She tells me the story of how Lush came into being. Originally Mark Constantine and Liz Weir made their own products and sold them in places like women's institutes, after they had first given talks. After a while they approached The Body Shop and Anita Roddick 'gave a break to the hippie who came in'. The products they made were among the most successful sold by The Body Shop, so Anita Roddick bought them out. With the money they gained Mark and Liz, with Mo Constantine, set up Cosmetics To Go, a mail order company selling their products. The products were great, but the organization and luck were less good. Cosmetics To Go went bust.

In time a new company rose from the ashes. But what to call it? They put the question to customers who came up with lots of product names as well as the eventual brand name. Apparently Mrs Elizabeth Bennett, without pride or prejudice, submitted her winning entry from Edinburgh. Lush it was.

As with Innocent, there is much in this story of the original founding of the company that shows the enduring tone and principles being set for the brand. If you read any copy of *Lush Times*, the paper distributed through Lush shops, you will see that many of the words and images are contributed by customers. And there is no dissonance of tone between the customers and the brand.

**Marni Griffin of Barton-upon-Humber passes on the Manifesto of her cats Coco and Queenie regarding Lush products:**

**We the undersigned Hereby PROTEST the Lush policy of not testing products on animals. How do you know a cat wouldn't like a nice bubble bath? The decision should be left up to us.**

The words, and the illustration that goes with them, are contributed by someone who uses Lush products. Products, such as, to give you just a random selection of names: Blue Skies & Fluffy White Clouds; God Save the Clean; Pink Caroline; I Should Coco; Happy for SAD Shower Gel; Angels on Bare Skin; The Ologist. Psychodelic is 'a bubble bath for complete nutters in the nicest possible way'. At Christmas time, Stocking Fellas are 'smelly things for men who wear tights'. Most brands would not give a second thought to names and descriptions like these. For Lush, and Lush customers, they fit absolutely. For me it is like overhearing a conversation from a girl's night out. There's a scatty zest about it but also a real sense that everyone involved in this conversation really cares for each other.

Sarah was herself a customer of Lush first, then was taken on to write the words. She combines this with teaching part-time at a business school while the Mafia, as she calls them, create the products and manage the business from the offices and factories in Poole in Dorset in the southwest of England. The Mafia is four people: Mark, Mo, Ro, and Helen. Mark, Sarah says, likes to 'work with the unemployable, bumping into the edges of acceptability'; he's also an international expert on birdsong.

If this all sounds incredibly hand-made, it is. But this hand-made business is now an international business. It has factories in Japan, Australia and Italy, all operating to the same principles. There is an obsession with raw materials. Fresh produce – orange, cucumbers, seaweed – arrives daily at the factories rather than tankers with chemicals. The seaweed comes from the Outer Hebrides, so does the water – the Poole water is not pure enough. The obsession with natural ingredients continues into an obsession with listing those ingredients with maximum clarity and visibility so that people know exactly what they are buying. Color-coding of the ingredients listed makes clear what is organic, what is natural and what is a safe synthetic.

Of course, it could all go wrong. Businesses can always go wrong. But Lush is very good at listening, and listening is a vital skill. It's the foundation of good writing as well as good marketing. It gives Lush adaptability to all kinds of market needs, so that when big businesses like Warner Bros wants a corporate gift for the re-release of Woody Allen's *Annie Hall*, Lush produces Annie's Hallsorts. But then turns the product into Coalface for selling in its shops the following year.

In the shops themselves the products are displayed with panache. Lush shops are a full-on experience. The smell of fruit and fragrant essential oils can be overpowering. In Newcastle in the north of England they had to seal up the ceiling because the tourist office above the shop complained about the strength of the smell. The colors, with slabs of soap in geological layers, are like those of Indian textile markets. And the words are shown with the same boldness. Words are on display everywhere, chalked on boards by one woman and an assistant to achieve consistency of style.

There are questions to be asked about the sustainability of this approach as the company gets bigger. But already Lush has a presence in some 20 countries and, by mail order, worldwide. No doubt there are strains, but the brand idea is strong, and it lives powerfully through its verbal identity. This is a company that cares obsessively about the things that are at the core of its brand: fresh, mainly natural ingredients; products that make you smile; a strong relationship with customers; honest and often funny words.

## Born to run

When Egg launched in the UK in 1997 it created quite a stir. This, apparently, was a financial services company. Called, for no reason that was obvious, Egg. It had some unusual advertising. And, when you dug a bit deeper, it was owned by the Prudential, one of the most staid and traditional companies in financial services. 'The man from the Pru' had come to represent everything that was old-fashioned about selling insurance, mortgages, pensions, and savings.

There was something else too. Egg had a way with words. For a financial company, it took risks with language. It even seemed to have a sense of humor and it didn't wish to hide it. But behind the jokes and the laddish language there was a determined idea about simplicity. Egg took trouble to explain. Where other financial companies confused customers with complex explanations, perhaps deliberately, perhaps unthinkingly, Egg went to great pains to be simple. Its simplicity seemed to me to go beyond 'Crystal Marks' and plain words which many banks had embraced as pointers to their 'customer focus'.

Five years on and Egg had survived. Indeed it had prospered. It seemed that its original belief in its own distinctive way with words had also survived and prospered. The newspapers reported improving financial results for the business; Egg agreed a deal to take over Zebank in France, making its first international expansion; and over 4 million people had become Egg customers.

I met Mike Harris, now chairman of Egg, and the man who had been brought in originally by the Prudential to run its new banking operation. So Mike had been there when Egg was just a light in his eye. The Prudential chief executive, Peter Davies, had started to get a little frustrated by what he saw as a slow pace of development for Prudential Banking. He asked Mike to take on direct distribution – by phone, internet, digital TV. In 1997 this was new stuff.

'I saw it as an opportunity to create a new organisation around the digital model. But I couldn't see any reason to do it as the Pru. Far from it. We had existing platforms we could use. The Prudential endorsement could be reassuring but it would not attract first movers itself. And I really thought it would be useful for the rest of the group – not in itself a reason to do it, but a good extra to have.'

The new business needed to appeal to people willing to experiment with a new kind of banking. Most transactions would be by the internet, not a trusted commercial medium at that time. There was research, as well as an instinctive belief, that the demand existed for smart, simple solutions in this market. But what to call this business?

'I'll take an awful lot of convincing,' said Peter Davies, 'that we should not call it Prudential.' Apparently there had been a substantial piece of work carried out into future customer needs, 'the world of the empowered customer'. This was a confident customer, not necessarily defined by age, who did not trust the existing banking infrastructure. The big banks, squeezing their costs, had started closing local branches without putting enough investment into new distribution channels. As a result, there was a wide discontent about the services of traditional banks. The 'new customers' were short of time and believed they could take care of themselves with only minimal help from their bank. And, almost by definition, this kind of customer was relatively well off. 'If you know you need to get your money sorted, you're almost certainly upmarket.'

Mike Harris believed his new operation needed a new name. It could not be Prudential. So he carried out some research which looked at three categories of possibility. The first category was a purely descriptive name. The second was an 'empty' name, a name with no inherent values (such as oxygen, 360°, ID). The third category was an off-the-wall name (like Yazoo or Popcorn). Most customers in research groups preferred the 'empty' category, without expressing a strong preference for any of the suggested names. Then the market researchers threw in 'Egg'.

'I said *no way*,' Mike Harris insists. 'But I was persuaded when they showed me the research results. Egg was the name everyone remembered.' Mike took the recommendation for Egg to the Prudential board, who threw it out. 'That would be very radical,' said Peter Davies. But one or two directors came up to Mike to say that the thinking was right – but 'stupid name'.

After this, Mike got even more determined. He commissioned further independent research and a month later went back to the board, saying 'it's got to be Egg'. This time Peter Davies and the board backed him. The name was laid.

'Something about the name Egg changed the nature of the conversations we were having. It was radical rather than merely intending to be radical. It fitted the values we had been talking about, but it demonstrated them too. We had been talking about dancing with customers as a way of showing a different kind of relationship, even though I don't think we quite pulled that off.'

Even if the idea of dancing did not quite happen, Egg held on to the founding principles. First, this was to be a digital operation – which was a shorthand term for a technology that would mean choice, convenience, quality and value for customers. Second, Egg would be a revolutionary force in finance, liberating people with smart, simple solutions. Honesty and simplicity were keys to the brand – and to the brand's language.

'We were very conscious of wanting to be coherent with the brand language. I think now it is very consistent. We'll say: here's a bunch of deadly boring but important stuff. There's edginess to the humor that can extend even to the small print. All this comes from the way we were thinking about it. The big driver was the need to be a revolutionary force, which we interpreted as not taking ourselves too seriously. The team started producing words, imagining the kind of language we might use. It got more formal – in the sense of being formalized – when the ad agency (HHCL) started writing things in April 1998.'

The first Egg ads featured celebrities like Olympic sprinter Linford Christie and radio and TV presenter Zoë Ball being interrogated in lie-detector tests. A key question was: 'Are you being paid to appear in this ad?' It reinforced the claim to invest in Egg because at least the ad was being honest about one of advertising's core dishonesties: celebrity endorsement. Then in subsequent advertising it continued this ironic game with the viewer/ potential customer. The presenter of one ad ends it with: 'I spent three years at RADA to reach this high point in my career.' In another ad, as children are shown walking past, the presenter says: 'They're not really children, they're child actors.'

As the business moves on things change, but some things stay the same. The executive committee has seven people, four of them founder members. These are people who remember going away for the weekends in hotels and imagining through words what Egg might be. The founding principles remain. The digital commitment remains the same, and the fact that most business is conducted on the internet has shaped the language, because it has enabled the language to be less traditional and formal. But Egg changed its ad agency recently because it felt that a smaller, younger agency (Mother) would better maintain Egg's edge as a challenger brand. 'And because we feel that, without losing edge, we need to be more inclusive.'

I came away with this final remark creating a question mark in my mind. Egg's advertising and language in its early days was refreshingly different. You could describe it as revolutionary. Other brands (Smile, for example) have now entered the market and started to encroach on Egg's territory. I wonder if Egg is becoming tamer and less differentiated, or whether the changed environment has made that seem so? So I go back to the website and some recent printed items.

**Email, phone or post**
**However you choose to talk to us, you won't**
**be baffled by complicated financial jargon.**

And, indeed, on the terms and conditions the heading says, '*Other stuff you need to know*'. But phrases like '*Our Key Features and Terms and Conditions are just made for each othe*r' remind me of a Lands' End catalog rather than Egg in its revolutionary origins. The website buttons – '*life's a picnic,*' '*don't slave, save,*' '*see the light,*' '*lovely supple figures,*' '*you're the big Kahuna, so delegate*' – have much more about them. Another leaflet divides into two parts – '*Here's the bit about servicing your accounts online*' and '*Here's the bit about servicing your accounts by phone.*' This seems honest, smart, simple. The language principles are maintained, even if they are not absolutely consistent. Even if they no longer seem quite as revolutionary as they once were.

My colleague Pete Dewar shows me an email he received about his Egg account. It's headed, '*In the words of David Bowie*' and starts, '*We've got some ch ch ch changes. We'd like to tell you about some changes to your Egg card, which will hopefully give you more flexibility and increased protection. In other words, they're good changes.'* I like the straightforwardness of that, perhaps more than the jokiness. And Pete tells me he appreciates Egg for being simple and friendly, rather than stuffy and serious – although sometimes the friend-to-friend language can grate. *'Oh, you're such a card,'* says the link to information about the Egg credit card. It's hard to pitch your jokes right when it's your customer's wallet you're holding.

In the financial marketplace the everyday language of Egg's approach is still refreshing. After all, we might be 'confident, empowered customers' but we still have too little time to puzzle our way through complicated financial information. We want finance to be made easy for us. We're people who can do sums but don't always understand the meaning of figures. So a passage like this from an Egg booklet is reassuring in its clarity:

**Get real**
**Rising prices can dramatically affect how your money grows.**

**Without understanding the effect of price rises, called inflation, it is hard to judge whether the risk you are taking is worthwhile.**
**Suppose a given investment promises to pay eight per cent, is that a good return?**

**If prices are rising at five per cent a year, your real return, the growth after inflation, is three per cent. But if inflation is ten per cent, then your money is actually losing value.**

**As a benchmark, you should be content to get a risk-free real return of two or three per cent a year. If you're going to risk capital, then look for a real return of at least four or five per cent a year.**

The language itself is straightforward and risk-free. Safe but comforting. Those are good qualities. But are they quite distinctive enough? The final section of the Egg booklet seems to be making a point that reaches beyond the subject of the guide ('investing with certainty') to a thought that underlies this book (embracing the excitement of discovering new things). So perhaps that is the best place to end this chapter's exploration, as we continue our journey and go in search of stories in the next chapter.

### . . . and finally

**No one can predict what the future will hold. While there are always going to be some risks in investing and in putting your money to work, remember that there are also risks in doing nothing at all. It is all too easy to find excuses not to act, and, before you know it, another year or two has slipped by. By reading this guide you have taken the first step to a more prosperous future.**

**Don't let it be the last.**

**Stories of exploration** 'Thou shalt not might reach the head but it takes Once upon a time to reach the heart.'
Philip Pullman

# The point of discovery

Our journey has taken us through the territory of brands that have established emotional links with customers through the power of their language. Perhaps significantly these are relatively new brands, able to speak in different ways to customers without the weight of their own histories acting as a brake on them. In doing so they have much to show older, bigger brands. Their words go beyond product information and beyond the creation of brand personality to tap into the power of storytelling. And they do so for customers outside and inside the company. For these brands have grown because they are driven by ideas that can be related to by those working inside the company – they still have founder members who are fiercely loyal to the original principles and legends. So, is there more in the idea of story that can help internal customers – employees, in particular – develop understanding of their brands? Can affection and loyalty grow from greater understanding? Let us see what we find when we move in this direction.

For many people the word 'story' conjures up regression either to an earlier time in the individual's life or to a previous era of human history. Whether from associations with childhood or mythological times, 'story' can evoke the impression of an emotional rather than an intellectual state of mind. As a result, in the business world, the idea of storytelling has been sidelined to the domain of the shaman not the management consultant.

In doing so, a terrible disservice has been done. A whole range of possibilities has been denied to people at work. In recent years this has started to change, but storytelling in business is still introduced with a defensive air of embarrassment or a shuffling of guilty feet.

But as the shelf starts to fill up with management books that sing the praises of storytelling, perhaps the subject is now entering the business mainstream. Yet different authors assign different meanings to the use of the word 'story'. A simple word, one of the first we understand as a child, is in danger of becoming a complex one. Steve Denning talks about how he used stories to achieve change in the World Bank. He calls his stories 'springboard stories' and argues convincingly for such stories to be minimalist and stripped of literary embellishment.

**The best way to explain it is through a story. In June 1995, a health worker in Kamana, Zambia, logged on to the Center for Disease Control Web site and got the answer to a question on how to treat malaria . . .**

That is the start of a springboard story, in just 30 words. The full story might be only ten times as long because Steve Denning is not interested in embellishing the story at the possible expense of deeper involvement by the listener in the creation of the story. He argues that for a story to be effective it needs the active participation of the listener. In effect, by listening, you tell the story to yourself in your own way – and that is when storytelling becomes really effective in bringing about change. It's a very disciplined, self-effacing approach for a writer to take and most writers have too great a love of language to embrace it.

It is simply one kind of storytelling that has worked in certain situations. There are many other kinds of storytelling. Rolf Jenson writes: 'Businesses need to imagine their futures the way that good novelists imagine their stories.' Products have stories behind them, and their stories provide the competitive edge. The company with the best story will win, because that story will connect emotionally with customers. 'Story' in this context comes close to meaning 'brand'.

These are valid uses of the word 'story' but my view is primarily a writer's view, albeit a writer who works in business consultancy. For me, stories have to be about the creative use of words which involves the stimulation of imagination and decisions about the exact choice of words. Otherwise we might just be talking about presentation techniques.

So, without disagreeing with these other definitions of storytelling, my view is that stories are actually much richer than those definitions might imply – and also have much greater potential in a business context. Stories succeed because they have the power to engage with people emotionally and that is the prime requirement of business today. To understand this, of course we need to discover more about the nature of storytelling.

**A great story transforms day to day living, inner and outer life, dream and actuality into a poem whose rhyme scheme is events rather than words – a two-hour metaphor that says: Life is like this!**

Robert McKee writes there about creating a screenplay but we can learn from every kind of storytelling. Indeed it's a skill that we learn at a very early age – just listen to and watch young children in a playtime break. Storytelling is an act of participation, involving teller and listener and, frequently, an exchange of those roles. Hence Steve Denning's emphasis on 'co-creating' a story.

Early stories are rudimentary because at a very young age we have little experience of life and we also have few memories. Memory is often the starting point for a story. Imagination cannot function without memory, without the store of past experiences to draw on. During workshops I have sometimes used an exercise that brings this out clearly. The exercise was suggested to me by seeing a performance by Simon McBurney of the Theatre de Complicité's play *Mnemonic*. Each member of the audience is given an airline mask and a leaf, and Simon McBurney then invites you back into your past by asking you to think of what you were doing at particular stages or key moments of your life. In the workshop I can dispense with the theatrical props but call on the same springs of memory. The effect is mesmeric and moving. But the point is that memory is telling the story. Or is it really your imagination?

But the story, having been imagined, is then much more memorable than other means that we might use to explain the world. From earliest times people have developed devices that aid memory and pass on knowledge from generation to generation. Among these are rhymes, songs, rhythm, pictures and stories. And perhaps story is the most important of these, because it lodges most vividly in our imagination.

In a sense we have reached a point of discovery. We are undertaking a journey in search of meaning, the aim of many quests. We seek simpler answers to make sense of a complex world; we look for truths that make greater sense of the confusion around us, so that we can understand better.

Stories provide us with a means to understand the world better and to understand the personal role we can play in it. A story is not written *about* you but *for* you. Each one of us reads something of our own story in any story written about someone else. Robert McKee says: 'Stereotypical stories stay at home, archetypal stories travel.' This means that, first, the archetypal story takes us to a world we do not know and, second, to a place we can recognize we might have been.

**Fiction gives life to form.**
*Jean Anouilh*

Stories are the way we make sense of the world, and stories give meaning to brands. The brand world is a world that needs stories and meaning. My colleague Mark Griffiths talks about 'every day grappling with meaninglessness'. That's an ironic phrase, particularly in the context of the situation he is describing, having to interpret other people's definitions of what a brand stands for. The truth is that, in trying to define what a business is really about, and what a particular brand really represents, people use words that can be vacuous. Vacuous and repetitive. I've grown particularly frustrated at definitions of brand values such as 'passionate', 'intelligent', 'determined', 'empathetic'. These are all worthy concepts but they are worthy only if they contain real meaning.

As brand consultants we try to imbue meaning into these words, but the words themselves are not enough. 'Passion' can mean something different for me than it means for you. And change the context, the culture, the environment, the language itself, and the meaning is forever shifting. So we need in some way to fix the meaning, to demonstrate such concepts more clearly, and stories are the most effective way to do that. Without the real story behind the word, 'passion' can mean something more likely to appear in a Jackie Collins novel.

A little while ago Interbrand held its annual conference in Berlin. The conference was organized by Interbrand's Swiss and German offices to share knowledge and discuss issues related to branding worldwide. The organizers decided that the conference should explore issues of identity. To do that, there should be a theme of 'crossing cultural boundaries', exemplified by the visual symbol of a hat. People attending from 24 different offices worldwide, brand consultants all, were asked to draw and bring with them a hat that expressed their individual identities.

I sense some blank looks out there. Some puzzled expressions. I was puzzled too. Then I was asked if I could write a story to express this theme. It should be a mystery of some kind, I was told. No problem there, I thought. The intention was that this story would be left in the rooms of delegates each evening before they went to sleep – three chapters over three evenings.

I talked about this with Mark Griffiths and it struck a bit of a nerve with us. We wanted to write the story, but we wanted the story to be seen as more than just a bit of light relief – for our own sakes, at least. We wanted to give the story some meaning about our own practice as brand consultants because of our concerns about daily 'grappling with meaninglessness'. For us, the great danger to be aware of is a tendency for brand to become bland – a tendency that could be accentuated by people coming together to share case studies as 'best practice'. There was a need, we felt, for a more skeptical antidote if we were to encourage challenging thinking on behalf of our company and our clients.

So we discussed what the story might be. I had long been a fan of Raymond Chandler novels. His work is familiar to people not just through the books but also through various film versions, particularly when Humphrey Bogart played the hard-boiled private eye, Philip Marlowe. And, of course, the character is famously identified by the wearing of a trilby hat. You might say his hat is his trademark. Suddenly we understood more vividly what our German colleagues intended by using the hat as a metaphor for identity.

We did some research on the internet, looking particularly at Berlin, the setting for the conference.

We know it as an atmospheric place, at least in our imaginations, and a mystery story needs a strong sense of location. We printed out a map of Central Berlin and discovered 'Los Angeles Platz'. That seemed to us the final pointer that we were on the right lines, the necessary bridge between the setting for Raymond Chandler's novels and the Berlin location for our pastiche story. Mark and I shared the writing, handing over sections to each other to take forward, discussing the direction of the story only in broad outline. The finished story follows, which we called *The Big It*.

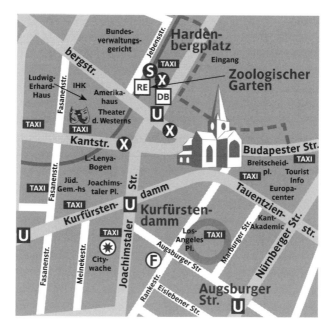

## The Big It
### *One*

*Picture our hero as the kind of Californian tough-talking, hard-drinking detective played by Humphrey Bogart in black-and-white films. But our hero, though wearing the same kind of trilby hat, lives in full color and has been sent to Berlin by his client Vandita Moynihan on the trail of . . . It. What is It? It's not clear to our hero, but he's keen to find out. His next pay check, perhaps his life, depends on it. It all seems to revolve around questions of identity and personal freedom, involving an international organization and an amazing collection of hats. Come with him to Berlin, where the mystery starts to unfold . . .*

I ignored the advice and jay-walked the lights over the Ku-damm, heading for a small book store on the other side of Los Angeles Platz. I was in a hurry and that's where she said I'd find It. I had the name of a store, Wittgensch & Nomura, the name of a woman, Hope Crouzet. But I didn't know what It was. Los Angeles Platz. I almost felt at home. Except the wind cut through my trench coat like a sharp metaphor. February, in Berlin. Brrr . . . and no way out of these unfamiliar city streets until I delivered It, gift-wrapped and gold-ribboned, right into her sophisticated, slim white hands back home in the hills above Central. Whatever It was.

Almost cut down in my prime by a seething Beemer driver, I swerved between a silver grey Jaguar XJS and a sleazy red Maserati stowed neatly against the kerb of a narrow one-way alley off Marburgerstrasse. It was that kind of district. She'd told me all sorts of stories about Berlin, but nothing had prepared me for it feeling just like home in an Ice Age. And she liked talking, did Vandita Moynihan.

I paused outside Wittgensch & Nomura's. I wasn't interested in the books. Books had never had time for me. I didn't have time for them. I was pretty sure they didn't contain what I was looking for. I wouldn't find It there. But I might find It here, inside the store. Besides, it was all I had to go on. So I was squinting through the dusky evening half-light, adjusting my trilby in the window.

Before I could check my beauty spot was still in the same place, the delicately paneled frosted-glass door burst open and crashed against the wall. I quickly pressed myself into the dim entrance-way of the apartment block next door. Out onto the quiet, murky pavement stumbled a tall, fashionably thin young woman sheathed in a leopard-patterned, knee-length dress that might have been one long tattoo. She was so well camouflaged, I couldn't see her face. But then my attention was distracted by the tight-suited mook who was strong-arming her out of the store and into the Jag. He had no small task. She fought like the cat she resembled. Her long, silky black hair scattered about her face and caught what little light was left. She was all thighs and claws on cream leather upholstery in the back of the car. Then, street silence.

Jammed into a small space next to entrance buzzers and lit panels with names like Fan-zhi, Schweitzer, Panini and Liebeck, I caught the heady whiff of chloroform. Soon, as if this was the way he closed shop each night, a small, middle-aged Italian-looking man, dapper-dressed with a tanned skin and silver hair beneath a flat cap, came out, straight as you like, triple-locked the door, walked calmly to the kidnap car, got in and drove north in the direction of the Zoologische Garten. I noted he hadn't slipped on his seatbelt. A professional driver.

I moved out of the shadows, picked up the small, black pill-box hat I'd seen leopard woman drop deliberately in the gutter, slipped it inside my coat, pulled up my collar and walked off west, towards the Ku-damm. Whatever It was, it had disappeared with the Jaguar. I didn't have It, but I did have a hat. Now I needed a drink.

## Two

*Our confused hero has witnessed the kidnapping of a beautiful woman he knows is at the center of the mystery. But who is she? To find out he'll have to find her, on a trail that will lead him into the middle of Berlin Zoo. There he'll overhear the sinister discussion of international agents on the brink of a scientific breakthrough that will change the world − for their benefit, of course, not ours. This could be It. The future of the world could be decided here. But that's still to come. First he needs a drink . . .*

I'd call it a bar if I was feeling polite. I hardly ever am. *The Chapeau Rouge* off Ranke Platz was the dive you find at the bottom of the deepest pool. It was damp, murky and it stank like last month's sauerkraut. But there were two things I needed. A drink and a place not to be seen. This dive suited me fine.

A double shot of Jack Daniels made me feel half-human but a second, followed by a beer, welcomed me back to the human race. I felt the lump under my coat and took out the hat the broad had dropped in the street. It was habit made me feel the lining. My fingers extracted the card with the name and address of the Zoo.

It wasn't far, and a cab dropped me at the gates in five minutes. This was one dark zoo. The jungle cats inside must feel at home. Except that the glimmer of light from the building might be keeping them up past their bedtime. I had to take a look. In Berlin, if there's a wall, you climb it. If there's a barrier, you cross it. It's part of city life. Ich bin ein Berliner. I went over the top and down the other side, landing on a pathway.

I was looking for It, but I didn't know what It was. I just had the idea It might be here. Lead on. I remember Vandita had talked about animals and I thought she meant her pooch not jaguars. OK, sometimes I'm wrong. The purring in the dark told me I was wrong.

It was one of those crazy buildings mad kings went away to for the weekend. I eased my way in through a side window and stole toward the hum of voices along an unlit corridor.

'. . . mais oui, c'est ca . . . '
'. . . das ist gut . . . '
'. . . molto con br . . . '
'. . . and we will . . . '

The Tower of Babel had nothing on these schmucks. Through the crack in the door I could see a dozen members of the League of Nations – they were that old too. Only two women, one a Hispanic type deep in conversation with a British version of Einstein. I could tell they were stitching up the meeting in advance.

'Gentlemen, ladies, let us begin. Herr Wittgensch. Nomura-san. Please take your seats. Welcome to our International Trade annual meeting. May I ask you to begin the meeting in the traditional way.'

My jaw fell open so fast I thought it would hit the floor. What the hell were they playing at? Every single one of them produced a bizarre hat from under the table and put it on. There was an ostrich-feather cap for the Spanish dame and a bowler for Einstein. A fez, baseball cap, beret, fedora, Easter bonnet, turban, Viking helmet, Russian fur, sombrero and a big-brimmed hat with dangling corks. All of a sudden I felt underdressed.

'We're here to consider the secret project that means so much to us all. Checkpoint Charlie we call it. My little joke. In a minute I will introduce you to our special exhibit that I know you're keen to see. Let's Hope . . .'

Outside it was pitch black. Suddenly here in the corridor it was full of stars. I'd got too caught up with the words of the joker inside the room. I hadn't heard the joker who came up behind me and slugged me on the back of the head. The stars blazed in my brain, it was almost pretty. I just remember thinking 'Auf wiedersehn. Adios. Adieu. Arrivederci. Goodnight Berlin.'

# Three

*Sore in the head, our hero regains consciousness in a locked room in Berlin Zoo. He finds himself locked up with the beautiful woman he had seen kidnapped. He knew she held the answer to It. What were the villains in hats plotting? He knew it meant no good to the rest of the world. He also knew the woman was key to their evil plans. What was her identity? Whose side was she on? Does she even have the heart to care? He knows the hatted group have their own self-absorbed agenda – but what is It? It's up to you to decide . . .*

It seemed this was the cage of a wild animal and I had woken up to find myself its captive playmate. My head was a drum beating out a syncopation straight out of downtown New Orleans. I was in no mood to dance but I didn't fancy lying down to dinner either. Lucky for the animal, who turned out to be the broad in the leopardskin dress. No self-respecting big cat would have worn one so tight, or could have.

Our cage was the deluxe upgrade of a broom cupboard. My head wailed jazz trumpet and my tight body was trussed up like an English chicken, back in the days when you could still get an English chicken. A small window in the room's slanting roof somehow caught the outer rays of a floodlight. It encouraged me to try opening my mouth.

'Hey, sister,' I called to the lithe form so near yet so strangely far away. 'What would it take to cut a man free? You look like you could do it with the whites of your eyes.'

True enough, I had no idea of the expression on her face. There was something about this woman that faded so easily into the background. It was almost inhuman. But her legs were straight out of Hollywood and her eyes had the gleam of a well-tended society girl. I followed the faint sheen of the long curve of her thigh. It seemed to produce the desired effect.

'Why should I?' she hissed. 'I've waited my whole life for this moment and nobody's going to take It away from me. Then all I want to do is rest.'

'What is It?' I asked, with all the nonchalance of a man on his way over to Alcatraz.

'If I untie you, promise you won't do anything rash,' she urged, moving towards me and flashing her thighs.

'In that case, you'd better untie my hands and blindfold my eyes,' I replied.

Then she told me, all right. International Trade was halfway through its plan to homogenize the world. Through subliminal messaging, they'd already persuaded half the world's male population to wear blue shirts. That's the way it was going. Now we were heading for the total eclipse of personality in which Hope Crouzet was to play the Sun and Moon rolled into one. It was all down to her and she was ready. She was their only hope, the only one of her kind in the world.

They droned on and on inside the hall, but Hope's monologue wore me down till I couldn't take any more. Only a day before, I hadn't even heard of It. Back in Central, Vandita had been so burned up by It, she couldn't even bring herself to say the word. But now I knew It wasn't a word. It was everywhere. It was in Wittgensch. It was in Italian. It was in this and every city in which I'd been unlucky enough to ply my trade. But I hadn't found It. It had found me. My mouth was dry. I licked my lips, then launched at her.

'Okay, cutie,' I said. 'We're all one cosy bunch of living, breathing, eating, sleeping, fornicating human beings, all right, but if I let you go in there and speak, it would be the end of millinery as we know it. No individuality, no culture, no imagination, no color, just one all-pervading corporate jambalaya. Everyone speaking interbranto and nobody wearing a hat ever again.'

Hope brought her face close to mine and pursed her lips. I could see right behind her eyes. Suddenly, I saw it all.

'Switch off,' I snapped at her. 'We're going out of that window if I have to drag you out by your tortoise-shell toenails.'

I pulled out my cell phone and let her have it right between the eyes with the full infra-red signal. Just as I expected, she became putty in my hands. I looked around the room. Stacked against the far wall in the gloom was a jumble of books nobody had touched since the days when politicians were honest. Their titles made me work even faster – *The world's greatest hats, Boshi, Boshi, Boshi, Keine Zukunft für Hutmacherhandwerk, We, me, them & hat*. At last I had found a use for books. I jammed several of each title up against the wall and dragged Hope up onto them. She was semi-conscious but this wasn't the first time she'd climbed out of a small window in a big hurry. It was all I could do to keep up with her. We were soon out, slithering over tiled rooftops, dancing in the shadows, bumping into polar bear cages and colliding with rhino compounds. It was a jungle in there. Then up and over the wire-mesh fence. Hope was quite an athlete. I was left gasping in her wake, not at all like a man looking up a woman's skirt with his mind on other things.

Out there, in the middle of Olof Palme Platz, I took a moment to take it all in. Me, a shamus on 100 bucks a day plus expenses, holding several million dollars on his arm. I put that arm around the greenbacks' shoulders. Now It was all mine. The Big It. Then, for some reason, I made as if to stroke the nape of her neck and pulled out the chip at the base of her hairline.

'Sei nicht traurig,' I said, turning to her lifeless form. 'It's better this way. Farewell my lovely. This is the rest you wanted. It's time for the long goodbye.'

Whatever made me leave the replicant standing there, like a statue in half-stride in the middle of the square, I'll never know. I guess that was just It. I tossed the chip into the silvery Spee. I didn't know what I was going to tell Vandita. I pulled my Trilby firmly onto my head and took the U-bahn east.

Many people no doubt dispensed with the story at the end of a long day of presentations and debate and a hard night of drinking. But many people read the story. We didn't point people to it to make sure they thought about its meaning. Stories work best when their meaning seeps into your consciousness without excessive rationalization. By their nature, stories connect in ways that appeal at an emotional level.

There are important implications in this, particularly for internal audiences. As individuals, working for brands and companies, we can naturally bring our own personalities to work. Indeed, if we do so, I believe the result will be more vibrant, appealing language when we write. But we are also aware of a 'corporate personality' that is available to us, perhaps demanded of us. Given a set of 'commandments' to follow, the most pliable of employees might plot small acts of resistance. Yet, given a deeper understanding of a brand's real values through storytelling, there is a much stronger possibility that an individual will be able to draw links and feel resonance between the corporate and the personal. Because a story invites each individual to find their own meaning within the framework of the shared story.

## Stories as starting points for brands

I started to wonder whether stories could achieve different purposes in different situations. There was a great lesson for me in the writing of the Berlin story. Storytelling is a powerful tool for defining and expressing business ideas – in particular, in the context in which I work, for giving greater meaning to brands.

Now this was not a blinding flash of light. In *We, me, them & it* I had called one chapter 'Telling stories'. There I had given some examples of stories used to help create companies and brands – for example, the invented Greek myth of Lumino (for a lighting company) and the folk tale of Barrington Stoke (for a children's book publisher). These might be described as original storytelling to create a brand – because they were very much to do with establishing the origins of the brand and showing through the story the principles that created and would drive the brand. These invented stories expressed a real truth about the brand and its founders. So clearly here is one category of storytelling in relation to a brand, and surely there must be others?

As I thought further about this purpose for story-telling, it seemed to be supported by the examples I had been researching. The 'yes/no' bins story, for example, tells you most of what you need to know if you are to get closer to the Innocent brand. It works so well because it has the absolute ring of truth.

It works better than this story I invented for a worldwide roofing company, coming together under a new name, Avius.

*What is the meaning of Avius? We have to take you back to the 14th century, to medieval Germany and the central Rhineland.*

*Avius was a small village in the region, not famous, not distinguished in any way. Like many other villages then and now it was situated in a valley, close to the river Rhine.*

*One winter there was almost constant rain. The rain lasted for weeks and weeks, the river swelled, people built the riverbanks higher. In the middle of one more stormy night the Rhine suddenly burst its muddy banks, submerging the village of Avius in the raging floodwaters. The village houses were swept away, its inhabitants were drowned in the flood – except for one man and one house. This was the only house in the village that was built of brick and stone. The man who lived in the house, who had built the house himself, was named Johannes. He climbed onto the roof of the house, the only part that remained above water.*

*Eventually the waters receded and Johannes was saved. Avius itself disappeared without trace. No one knows its exact location, and Avius has achieved a legendary status like a domestic version of the lost kingdom of Atlantis. The legend has it that Johannes became a monk, renowned for his architectural skills. Different countries and monastries claim association with Johannes, and architectural drawings have been discovered in Italy and France with the signatures of Giovanni da Vius and Jean d'Avius.*

*Today Avius lives on, not just in our imagination but in reality.*

From the story you might gather some essential messages about roofing, protection, craftsmanship and a company with European origins. The story, though, will not be used as the brand legend in the way that the Innocent story has been. It does not spring out of reality in the way that the Innocent story does. It was created as a way to understand that the brand name could adopt a richer meaning than the abstract name might suggest.

But the most powerful stories of brand origins will normally be those that have the ring of truth. Business people are wary of stories because there is something deep in our upbringing that says 'stories are not true.' A mother will tell her child 'not to tell stories' – not to tell untruths or fibs. It's a difficult argument, therefore, to persuade business people, who love facts, evidence, analysis and measurement, that the way to understand and express deeper truths about their business is through stories. But that is my contention. Stories enable real connections to be made with audiences, reaching to a deeper level of reality than the usually bland statements of corporate description.

I discovered the truth of this initially many years ago, when I first entered the world of identity consultancy. In interviewing people in companies, I simply had to listen to what people wanted to tell me. They all told me their stories. The stories of how they joined the company. What happened to them. How they first came across it. What their day consisted of. What they told the customers. How the company made decisions. How it told good or bad news. What the company is really all about.

Tell me, I said. And people did.

A story needs two people to engage with it. The teller and the listener. The writer and the reader. It's the surest way we make connections between people. A story depends upon participation but it is also the most effective way to ensure participation. And participation is what every brand wants. Every brand would like to be seen as a club that people aspire to join – a club whose philosophy you share, a place where you can go to be yourself and to meet other like-minded people, and an opportunity to talk and share stories. A club which allows you to be an individual within a communal framework, because we all need to assert our individuality, even – or perhaps especially – in a corporate context.

### Stories for personal expression

My argument for storytelling as a business tool goes beyond the uses of stories explored so far. Stories can help us to explain the origins of brands; to understand the real distinctiveness of a business; to communicate effectively between individuals.

It seems to me almost a truism to say that people need to find and use their own voices to communicate well. People enjoy telling stories, but most of the time they are denied the opportunity to do so. They are denied because there is a puritan school of management, a philosophy that has prevailed for most of the last century. This philosophy says that self-expression at work is time-wasting self-indulgence. Fortunately, for the job satisfaction of all who work, this is changing.

A constant theme of the way I practice my consultancy is to encourage people to bring more of their personalities to work – and to give expression to that in their writing. What is the purpose of this? I could say that I believe in adding to the sum of human happiness because that would be a noble goal in itself. But I can hear business braces twanging in my head. Not good enough. Yet, a part of me protests, that really is *more* than good enough. Any business has an interest in helping its employees to work effectively. If those employees are content with themselves, they are more likely to be content with their work, and more likely to perform their jobs well.

This philosophy lies behind most of the workshops and writing programs I have carried out for various clients over many years. There is a simple principle that people will write better if they enjoy writing. Pleasure is a useful principle at work. Writing is a vital aspect of work because, for many people at work a key task is to persuade and influence others. You need words to do this, you need to develop writing skills if you are to be an effective persuader.

Lever Fabergé, part of Unilever, recognized the truth of this. They also recognized the need to help their own people express their creativity if they were to become a more genuinely creative company – and they had expressed that as one of their corporate goals. At first I became involved in an extraordinarily bold and imaginative program called Catalyst. This was the idea of Alastair Creamer who introduced a mixture of artistic activities and stimuli to Lever Fabergé. There were various aspects of the program, encouraging people to engage with visual, performance, musical and literary arts. For example, collaborating with Helen Storey on the design and execution of an art installation / sculpture; masterclasses with the jazz musician Andy Sheppard; playwriting workshops at the Royal Court Theatre.

For six months, as part of Catalyst, I was writer-in-residence for one of Lever Fabergé's key categories, 'deodorants and grooming', alongside the poet-in-residence, Jackie Wills. Our group comprised 35 people who were responsible for managing brands like Sure, Impulse, Dove. The group was headed by Steve Miles, a Lever Fabergé director, who was himself passionate about writing and who had a belief in the potential of stories and poetry to help the individuals in the business.

We gathered on a spring day in 2001 in a country house off-site that was packed with sculpture, icons, works of art, and set in beautiful gardens. It was important to send an immediate signal that we were intent on taking people outside their normal experience of work. On that first day we read poems and stories, we tried writing exercises, we made paper notebooks by hand. Then over the next six months, for about one day a week, Jackie and I worked with the team, individually and in different combinations of groups.

Our aim was to build confidence in people's ability to express themselves in writing. If we could achieve that we believed that the effects would be felt by the business through the documents, reports, proposals, briefs and letters that the team would write outside the program. We deliberately avoided making everyday business-writing the focus of our coaching, while constantly bearing in our minds that people would return to their desks to do that kind of writing. But, for the space of a morning or afternoon, we wanted to liberate people from the need to write for and about the business.

Over the next six months we encouraged the team members, through a variety of exercises, to express their own personalities in their writing. We were impressed by the consistently high quality of the work produced. To recognize this, I persuaded Steve Miles that we should produce a book that marked the residency, reminded people of what they had done, gave tips to keep in mind and, most important of all, published examples of the writing produced by the team members.

There is nearly always a business demand to measure the effectiveness of any program. But this program was impossible to measure. We believe it improved writing skills; we believe it made the team more confident in their own creativity; we believe it motivated people and helped team morale. But we have no figures to prove this. The best measure we have are the examples of writing produced by the team.

I'm sure most of the team were skeptical when we began. Here we were introducing poems and stories into the working day. Perhaps the first issue was simply 'how to read a poem?' This poem by the US Poet Laureate set the scene.

I ask them to take a poem
and hold it up to the light
like a color slide

or press an ear against its hive.
I say drop a mouse into a poem
and watch him probe his way out,

or walk inside the poem's room
and feel the walls for a light switch.

I want them to waterski
across the surface of a poem
waving at the author's name on the shore.
But all they want to do
is tie the poem to a chair with rope
and torture a confession out of it.

They begin beating it with a hose
to find out what it really means

*Billy Collins*

We then got people writing both openings and endings to novels, writing them in the style of different writers. People on the team were always surprised by how well their colleagues performed these exercises. Respect for each other spread around the group.

Metaphors can be like tiny stories. Put together a string of metaphors and you can build up a vivid picture of a person you are describing. Using a Simon Armitage poem 'Not the furniture game' as stimulus, people wrote metaphors line by line and then discovered that they had written poems. We asked people to have a real person in mind, a consumer of one of their brands, and then to respond spontaneously to our promptings by writing down metaphors. Here are two examples, which contain real insights.

John 25

He is a Vauxhall Astra. 2 ltr. Quick, but not too flashy.
Plenty of boot space for kit and for golf clubs. Red.
  No Gimmicks.
He is seven in the morning.
He is the colour of health club swimming pools.
He is a changing room bench, with lockers
  behind him.
He is a clean smell, the smell of someone who has had
  a shower and cleaned themselves with basic soap.
He is an unfashionable county near London.
He is the texture of the grips on a weight machine.
He is a hooded top with the name of a local sports
  club on it.
He is a banana, basic. One of a bunch.
He is the sound when you're running and your
  tape stops and you can suddenly hear your
  feet hitting the ground and your lungs working.

*Tom Swift*

Jeannine (the Impulse girl)

She is a strapless top thrown over the back
   of a chair
She is the first car which kangaroos down the street
She is the hawthorn blossom in the hedges
She is the sweet, long cocktail left on the bar
She is first thing in the morning when it is still sunny
She is the blue of the sky and the black of a
   Doc Martens boot
She is the Spanish Costa in the sunshine
She is the hope of a red rose wrapped in cellophane
She is the giggle on the back of the bus.

*Kathryn Robinson*

Simple, mundane techniques – making a list, for
example – can be transformed by a little care. We asked
people to write lists of the contents of their pockets,
cases or handbags. The results were surprisingly poetic
but also gave you a real sense of the individual writer's
personality. Here are two examples.

   4 credit cards, 3 Swiss francs, 2 broken combs
      and a pair of sunglasses with one leg.
   9 grotty tissues, 3 fuzzy bands, 2 leaky biros
      and one current agenda (carefully hidden)
   3 sad tictacs, 2 escaped tampons, 2 lovers' numbers
      and one little bag of daydreams

*Kathryn Robinson*

A pen that is forever handy
A photo that will always bring out a smile
That money note from a foreign country to
    bring back fond memories.
A perfume card with your favourite scent
Your credit card and cash for those impulse
    purchases,
A brolly – if you're in England –
Some powder to touch-up and go,
A brush to keep you looking on form,
Your mobile – an ever essential item,
Lipgloss and a Band-Aid

Oh, and finally, don't forget your keys.

*Georgina Jenkins*

At other times people adopted an opposite discipline.
Rather than the discursive list, in which we encouraged
people to put everything down, we then turned to
the minimalistic, compressed form of the haiku. Our
challenge was to say what you do – in your working life
– in three lines with a set number of syllables. These
become mini-stories.

'Director', as in
A conductor – fronting up
Thirty-five talents


I'm a peeping Tom
A detective and a spy
All rolled into one

I'm the secret aide
Pushing the edge in small ways
Forcing renewal.

The haiku form almost forces people to write in a way that is completely different from 'business speak'. But at the same time it imposes disciplines – brevity, precision, word selection – that are fundamental to good business writing.

Not everything worked. We didn't always have groups bubbling over with enthusiasm. Sometimes there was resistance. Often people wondered if they should be back at their desks doing 'real work'. And every so often people wondered about relevance. Once, people felt we were getting them to abandon all their safe rules and formulas – were we right to do so, was this really allowed? So, that day, I started the workshop on concept writing with these words. (A concept, in Lever Fabergé terms, is a description of a new product or brand variant that will be tested in market research.)

*First, concept writing is a form of creative writing – you're using words to create a picture of something that doesn't exist. To get to that final piece of creative writing, you need to go through a lot of creative thinking, so we were giving you some techniques both to think and write creatively.*

*In doing so, we were not saying reject all the existing rules, for example insight / benefit / reason to believe. One of my favorite quotations is Hofstadter's 'I suspect that the welcoming of constraints is, at bottom, the deepest secret of creativity.' It's a favorite because I believe in it – it's true.*

*Sometimes, though, we're constrained by unnecessary rules. These might be invisibly imposed by the organisation and the people who work inside it. They become real in our heads, and our thinking gets limited. The principles, designed to be helpful, become a formula.*

*So, what we need to do is two things simultaneously (which might seem contradictory, but I don't think they are):*

*We need to welcome the constraints (the briefs, if you like) and see them as a creative support.*

*We need to challenge constraints, in their wider sense, to see whether we need them and to explore whether we can break through to something that is more meaningful to us as individuals and also to the company and brands we work for.*

*What we were trying to do was to encourage you to welcome creative constraints and to challenge any unwelcome constraints (which might be self-imposed). Our objective was to help you produce more genuinely creative writing, based on creative thinking.*

Our program came to an end on an afternoon in early October that was National Poetry Day. The theme of National Poetry Day in 2001 was journeys. We asked each member of the team to select a poem about a journey (physical, mental, spiritual or of any kind). We gathered as a group and everyone attended. Then we asked people to read aloud the poems they had brought. It was a moving experience to listen to 35 individuals reading poems of great diversity. We concluded with a poem that Jackie Wills had written for the day, but my favorite poem by Jackie was written in response to the name of a new fragrance, Moon Grass, developed for Impulse.

The moon's a golf course

An expert perfumier who can mimic
the scent of a baby, tells me a rose
grown in space smells of distilled water.
Its petals unwrap in pure oxygen, free
of heavy metals. Inhaling deeper
he detects a moon covered in turf,
cropped close and springy,
which doesn't shine. Ah, he says,
the moon's a golf course; in the night
sky, a button on your web page.

*Jackie Wills*

That poem starts to suggest how the benefits of the residency might feed back directly into the team's work. Here we were enabling people to see their work and their brands in a different light. They discovered that they really could tell stories and that through those stories they could achieve personal insights. More than that, they could share those insights vividly with others. That is the magic of storytelling. Perhaps, most importantly, they were able to use poetry and storytelling to make the connection between two worlds – the individual and the corporate.

### A story is a tightrope between two worlds.
*Jeanette Winterson*

Storytelling provides that connection between two people, between teller and listener, writer and reader, individual and employee, brand and customer. There are many possible points of connection. The real power of a story is that it enables any number of different connections to be made. This can be particularly crucial in a world where one of the worst possible mistakes is an obvious separation between 'them and us', between the cold distancing of bureaucracy and the warm proximity of the personal.

## Stories to clarify and inspire brands

Stories can do many things but for me they always need to be written with some emotion. The language we use conveys or betrays emotion; and I always look for genuine emotion in the words that I read or hear, and I usually try to insert emotion into the words that I write. I believe it's what we all seek, if only because it makes our lives more interesting.

Of course, there are always examples of writing that has had every last drop of emotion wrung out of it. Even a brand like Virgin, that is perceived to be 'of the people', can be let down by an individual spokesperson. When asked why trains had skipped stations and stranded passengers to make up for the lost time, Virgin was reported as saying:

**This is to minimize customer disbenefit.**

The language of bureaucracy has a long history too. Shakespeare invented – or did he borrow? – a word whose only recorded use is in *King Lear*. Lear's daughter Goneril says: 'I beg you to disquantity a little.' By using 'disquantity' – it didn't catch on – Shakespeare is letting us know not only that Goneril is a heartless daughter but also an insensitive bureaucrat.

Bureaucracy creates its own language, and bureaucratic language aims to cast a fog over meaning. When we come across such language, we resent the attempt to disguise meaning and we react against the brand represented by such language. The bureaucratic voice of the Tube writes on a white board:

**London Underground regrets the disruption caused by industrial action.**
**We have done everything possible to minimize your inconvenience.**

Emotion, beyond a tone of tetchy exasperation, has been excluded, to leave passengers dissatisfied because the bureaucratic language also tries to exclude us from involvement in the experience itself. But, at its best, the Tube can have a personal tone if a driver recognizes that the journey is a shared experience and speaks on the intercom when the train is stuck in a black tunnel:

**I'm sorry for the long delay. I'm told there was a queue of trains at Arnos Grove.**
**I do understand your frustration and I'm frustrated myself because when I get to Arnos Grove I can go home too.**

In this example, the driver shows he understands the stories of individual passengers – 'I'm late, I'm tired, I'm hungry and I want to get home' – and invites passengers to understand that he shares the story.

There is no excuse for a 21st-century business to retreat into bureaucratic language. But in saying so I am implying that earlier generations of business people were more inclined to bureaucratic language. Perhaps they were, but not in all cases. In Victorian times the novelist Anthony Trollope had a senior job at the Post Office. Nowadays we might call him a 'customer service manager' – but of a very active, dynamic kind. In looking at ways to improve the Irish postal service he checked every postal round in Ireland and brought in many improvements that its modern-day equivalent is busy retreating from. He also stuck to a firm principle when writing his reports to the Post Office and its director Rowland Hill. His dedication to this horseback consultancy delayed his own literacy activities but, given the eventual volume of his fictional output, not too seriously. He had, he wrote, 'a thorough love of letters – I mean the letters which are carried by the post.' His aim was to write official reports that 'were pleasant to read'. Oh for more Trollopes in public service companies today.

The point is that Trollope knew how to tell a story and, without ever using or knowing such a term, he understood the brand he worked for. He certainly understood that language was integral to it and that engaging language tells the story best. Yet the story has to have content and a real purpose, as Thomas Hardy wrote only a little later:

**A story must be exceptional enough to justify its telling. We storytellers are all ancient mariners, and none of us is justified in stopping wedding guests, unless he has something more unusual to relate than the ordinary experiences of every average man and woman.**

Hardy's words apply when we tell stories that aim to explain extraordinary brands. And what genuine brand does not consider itself extraordinary? Let me tell you the story of my telling of the Guinness brand story.

I grew up in a family that enjoyed social drinking. I have early memories of sitting on pub doorsteps while my mother had a drink with friends or family. This was certainly not a case of child neglect, because I enjoyed the lemonade I drank while my mother had her Guinness inside the pub.

Because of this experience, Guinness was one of the first brand names that meant anything to me. I associated it with my mother who remained a Guinness loyalist all her life. Even though I did not become a regular Guinness consumer when I reached drinking age, I always felt great affection for the brand.

It was a surprise and a delight then, when I was invited to write the stories of the Guinness heroes. I was approached by Jon Potter, global brand director for Guinness, who was convinced of the potential for stories to bring fresh clarity and vigor to the brand. Jon had led the team that was defining the Guinness brand in a way that would unite Guinness's heritage with its future direction, and creating one global positioning in the original territories (Ireland and the UK), established markets (USA, the former British colonies) and developing regions (especially Africa and southeast Asia). Guinness meant different things in each of these areas, so it had been a difficult task to gain acceptance that there was a single brand idea behind Guinness.

However, Jon had succeeded in that. The brand idea was defined as 'inner strength'. Future advertising would demonstrate that Guinness is the brand that gives you inner strength. This could exhibit itself as a quiet but confident self-belief or as a bullish determination to succeed.

But Jon believed firmly that this was not a new invention of the Guinness brand. All that his team had done was to dig deep and discover the original essence of Guinness. The principles on which the company and the brand were first founded must surely have contributed consistently to Guinness's success over two and a half centuries. Was this true? If so, could we find and tell the stories that would demonstrate it?

Mark Griffiths and I went off to Dublin, delighted to be let loose in a brewery. We spent our time there speaking to people with long Guinness associations and memories; and we visited the archives. The main Guinness archives are based in the Park Royal site, in West London. There is an extraordinary wealth of historic material relating to the development of the company, particularly its marketing and advertising activities. Because it is a well-loved brand, and because the Guinness family have played notable roles in British and Irish politics, there are also many books about all aspects of Guinness.

By this point, though, we were in danger of drowning in a vat of Guinness information. We did not want to write the history of Guinness; nor was that what Jon Potter wanted. But we had histories, memories, names and images filling our brains, so we needed to find a way of distilling this. The key was to remind ourselves of the original impetus that had come from Jon Potter. He wanted to know the stories that show Guinness has always been the brand for inner strength.

It was clear that we had to start with the founder himself, Arthur Guinness. So I wrote a short introductory story that would set the scene for a longer account of the company's early years. In a little office in Park Royal, I read out the following story prologue to Jon Potter and Francis Eames, who had been our guide to the Guinness history.

*The story starts with the expletives deleted. We don't need to sanctify the memory of our founder but no one ever recorded the swear words Arthur Guinness flung across the barricades at the gentlemen from the Dublin Corporation in 1775. But fling them he did.*

*The temptation is to describe Arthur Guinness as a stout gentleman. Well, we make no point about his girth but we do know that Arthur Guinness took his time before he came around to brewing porter. When he finally did it, it was worth waiting for.*

*But it was water that did it. The whole history of Guinness is built on water.*

*Think of that the next time you sink a pint. If Arthur hadn't made his first stand against the bureaucrats and stood up for his commercial rights we wouldn't be here now thinking of new ways to fight the Guinness cause.*

*'I did a deal, dammit, so let's stick to it!'*

*Arthur stuck to it. It took him twelve years to win his fight for the Dublin water rights, but he won. And that was the first crucial turning point in the story of Guinness.*

*It takes strength to do it. Not necessarily the girder-lifting strength of a strong man, but the commitment that comes with an inner certainty.*

*Think about it. Savour it. And lift your glass to Arthur. We owe it to him.*

The drama of my reading was either destroyed or heightened by the sudden clanging, halfway through the story, of the fire alarm. We all trooped outside for 15 minutes while, inside my head, I was imagining the expletives that Arthur might have used in this situation. When we returned inside, Jon asked me to read the story again. And this time there was no clanging of bells, just a quiet expression of satisfaction.

The story established the pattern for what now needed to follow. First, it made clear that each of the stories had to have a real person at the center, with honest human characteristics. No hagiography. Secondly it established the tone of voice, which drew on memories of phrases from Guinness's past advertising, and could be imagined as spoken with a very soft Irish accent. Thirdly it pointed to the narrative crux of each story, the need for each to have a resolution of conflict, the taking of a decisive action at a vital moment. This gave us a subtitle to the book: six turning points for Guinness that hinged on inner strength.

All that remained was to write the stories. We agreed the six subjects, based on our research, and we arranged to meet people who would be featured or would add personal knowledge to the stories. One of these people was Alan Wood, who would be a hero of the sixth story. He had been Guinness's advertising manager at a crucial time in the early 1960s and now he was a remarkably sprightly and dapper man in his late 80s. Another was David Hampshire, still active in the company, who had done an enormous amount to grow many markets for Guinness in Africa.

Through these stories, through delving into company history and listening to personal testimonies, we had discovered a remarkable continuity between the past, present and future of the Guinness brand. We could sense, from very limited trials with our main contacts in Guinness, that there was genuine excitement that these stories would prove revelatory and inspiring to all Guinness people who would read them.

The six stories were:

### The Founder's Tale
*Arthur Guinness and the company's early years*

### The Toucan's Real Tale
*Ben Newbold and Guinness's first venture into advertising*

### The Draughtsman's Tale
*Michael Ash and the invention of Draught Guinness*

### The Traveller's Tale
*Alan Lennox-Boyd and overseas expansion*

### The Widget's Tale
*Alan Forage and the development of the device
that made canned Draught Guinness possible*

### The Marketer's Tale
*Alan Wood in the 1960s and David Hampshire
for Guinness in Africa*

Here is *The Marketer's Tale,* with illustrations by
Robin Heighway-Bury.

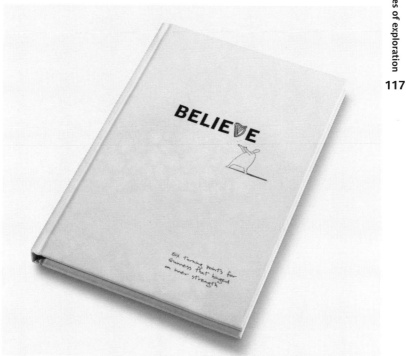

The Marketers Tale

# Who drinks Guinness?

No one knew until the first market research in the 1950s.

## The answer seemed to be: working men, getting on in life.

Deeper than that, though, the 'reparative theory' was born – in short, at the end of a hard day, you've earned that Guinness.

# But was Guinness still earning the market's support?

Sales were stagnant, even in decline. The advertising looked tired, outdated in the new TV age. Gilroy's menagerie had outlived their time. But it was a big decision to turn against what the public, ad agency and the Guinness board loved for all the wrong reasons.

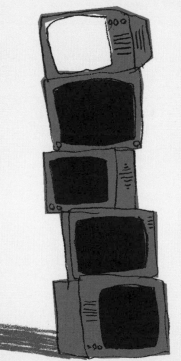

Complacency had set in, so any challenge to the Guinness way of advertising was a big challenge.

**Who would argue the case for radical change when everything was stacked against him?**

Alan Wood was the man, Guinness's Advertising Manager in the 1960s, an elegant iconoclast, a courteous rebel. And, in doing so, he put Guinness back on the path to growth. Sales of Guinness soared, the brand was forever synonymous with bravery in advertising.

**Alan's courage meant that he made it possible for future generations of marketers to be brave too.**

# Cheers, Alan Wood,
**you've earned the thanks of Guinness**

Put yourself back in time, to the late 1950s, so that we can sometime later in this story look forward. Go back in your imagination to a world where television was the bright new medium — a medium that existed then only in black and white. A black and white world that seemed in danger of passing Guinness by.

Because, if the world had changed, it appeared that the Guinness company had not. True, Guinness Draught had just come along and it was going to do wonders for the long-term health of Guinness, given proper marketing support some years along the line. But look at the company itself, look at the image of Guinness and the Guinness drinker at that time. This process of looking, a perhaps overdue critical analysis, is what started to happen in the late 1950s. In 1955 Guinness had recruited a new Advertising Manager from outside the company.

Tommy Marks joined Guinness from British European Airways. He started to introduce some changes to the Guinness advertising but the basic approach was in the playful tradition established by John Gilroy, now reinforced by other distinguished artists such as Abram Games and Edward Ardizzone.

## There was a tangible feeling that things had to change – but how?

Even the new medium for advertising – television – saw animated versions of Gilroy cartoon animals rather than a creative rising to the fresh challenge.

# The question
## 'Who drinks Guinness?

Sales had grown until the mid-1950s, then they had
levelled off, and now, in 1959 they were in decline. For
the first time, market research was brought to the aid
of Guinness. It came initially from Gallup and Mass
Observation, then from Public Attitude Surveys, and for
many people in Guinness it was a strange mixture of the
reassuring and the disturbing. Reassuring that Guinness
had a high degree of loyalty among drinkers; disturbing
that its loyal core was overwhelmingly male and advanced
in years (average age 55). The danger for Guinness was
that its drinkers were ageing and its image was ageing
with those drinkers.

## Something needed to be done.

Recalling those days, with the benefit of hindsight
of course, everyone agrees that the response, when
it happened, was remarkably swift. Brendan Nolan,
who had just arrived at the ad agency Benson's, observed:

## "The change in Guinness advertising happened almost overnight."

The main reason was the arrival at Guinness of a new
Advertising Manager, Alan Wood, recruited from Rank
Hovis McDougall.

Alan Wood came in and he knew that action was needed.
He learnt the deeper lessons from the research. Above all,
he sought the strengths to build on. The research categorised
drinkers into three groups which Alan Wood recalls:

"First there were people who drank for
reasons of fashion.

Secondly there were those who drank
for oblivion.

And thirdly there were those for whom
drinking was an important part of their
life; a habit and a reward for effort."

**This third group became known
as 'reparative' drinkers.**

Like a morning cup of tea, a drink has almost
a ritualistic appeal for this group. And, interestingly
for Guinness, these were clearly the Guinness drinkers.
There was an appealing idea, based on the reality of
research with drinkers, that a glass of Guinness could
be seen as something that you deserve because you have
earnt it through your efforts during the day.

Alan Wood seized on this idea. For him it had the additional appeal that there seemed a clear link with Guinness's first advertising.

# 'Guinness is good for you'

had been the original slogan, derived at the time from 'research' carried out by Benson's, who had spoken to drinkers in pubs. This line had been supported by the endorsements of real doctors. Now far more rigorous research suggested that the 'reparative theory' – belief in Guinness's ability to put something back that a hard day had taken out – had a deep level of support among consumers.

But not everyone trusted research. And there was still a tremendous emotional attachment to the style of Guinness advertising represented by John Gilroy thirty years after its original creation. For Benson's, who had been Guinness's only ad agency, there were some difficult pills to swallow.

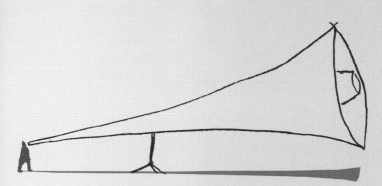

David Ogilvy, who worked on the Guinness account
when it was won by Ogilvy & Mather many years later,
had warned against using research "as a drunk uses
a lamp post. For support not illumination." Here,
though, was illuminating research that Benson's met
with suspicion. Alan Wood needed to win them over.
In particular he needed to convince Bobby Bevan, the
chairman of Benson's and a copywriter himself, that
**Guinness needed to listen and learn,** and then make
a bold change of style. No doubt Bevan was worried
about this upstart newcomer, this Guinness outsider
who now threatened the advertising heritage that
Benson's had created for Guinness. He took soundings
from people who had worked previously with Alan Wood.
And gradually the ice thawed.


**Respect developed.**
**The two men became good friends.**
**And the advertising changed.**

It changed in perhaps the most startling way of all. It now relied on absolute simplicity and clarity. Some thought it boringly simple. Alan Wood thought it single-minded, and that reflected his conviction at that time.

The style reflected his first rule of advertising:
'Never advertise an undrinkable drink.'

Or, to see it another way, always advertise to make your drink look supremely drinkable. His criticism of recent Guinness advertising had been that it had become like a cult, jokiness had become an aim in itself, it was advertising that appealed to people who liked advertising. He wanted advertising for people who liked a drink; a drink of Guinness. Guinness, the product, became the undoubted hero of the new advertising.

It had been one thing to persuade the ad agency to shift its position. Alan Wood knew that it might be even more difficult to persuade the Guinness board. The board at that time was made up almost entirely of Guinness family members – and of those the complaint from some quarters was that there were 'too many fur coats'; female members of the aristocratic Guinness family, suspected for knowing too little about the product and business.

Alan Wood and the board were not well-known to each other. Wood knew that the board were conservative by instinct and upbringing. They would probably see change as a risk; they might well see radical change as a threat to their whole set of beliefs and values. As he waited nervously to be called to the meeting, Alan Wood would have rehearsed the arguments, but these were arguments that he knew well, and believed in. Besides, he had a natural charm and an easy manner – and, now he looked at them, he realised with a slight misgiving that he also had a remarkably small collection of visuals for a year's ad campaign, each visual a minor variation on the previous one. Each ad showed a bottle of Guinness and a glass, beautifully photographed, and a simple headline.

**GOOD FOR YOU**

**Where, the board might ask, is the fun in that?**

Of course, he also had the research as back-up to the advertising, and an important element in Alan Wood's new approach to advertising was the use of research before, during and after campaigns. For the first time, Guinness would actually measure the effectiveness of its advertising against objectives that went beyond 'Have we sold more Guinness?' Alan Wood engagingly admits that the meeting with the board was 'tough'. He presented his arguments, then he showed the advertising. There was silence and a wall of stony faces around the table. You could feel the tension in the air. The silence was eventually broken – the delay might only have been seconds but it felt like minutes – by Lady Honor Svedjar, daughter of Rupert Guinness.

I'm sorry, but I have to go. I will just say that I have heard a lot of common sense here. It has my support.

With that, Lady Honor, one of the 'fur coats', gathered her papers and left. She had made the first and crucial judgement, the tension was broken, the day was won and the board approved the new advertising.

**It took courage to do what Alan Wood did, but for Guinness it certainly paid off.**

Sales of Guinness picked up and they set off on a path of growth. Research showed that the age profile for Guinness drinkers was much lower as a result of the new advertising. And a new but permanent playing field for Guinness advertising and the Guinness brand had been established. On this playing field, there was no longer any room for complacency; there was simply the recognition that the team needed to be brilliant and

**the team needed to believe in itself.**

Alan Wood brought in a succession of new campaigns through the 1960s. He also brought in consistent elements of the visual identity; colour scheme, typography, a standard way to write 'Guinness' rather than the 17 different ways that had previously existed. The basis for a global brand was being laid.

In all this, Alan Wood was a pioneer. He went on to play a leading role in Guinness's development internationally. But most importantly he gave an example that we can still draw on when we come to critical points in business development. Let us take two later examples of Guinness responding to marketing challenges at key turning points of history, examples which adopt the spirit and belief shown by Alan Wood.

In the mid 1980s Guinness was going through a turbulent period of its history, involving bids and takeovers. And the 'Genius' advertising campaign had received a mixed reception. Again there was an almost tangible sense that change was needed in Guinness's advertising approach.

## Enter the 'Man with the Guinness'

The 'Man with the Girder' had appeared in the 1930s, the first personification of the Guinness brand. But now, for the first time, there was a real human brand icon for Guinness in the mysterious form of Rutger Hauer, a man in black with a blonde head.

In his early days, David Hampshire learnt a lot from Alan Woo

# "Sell a bit of Guinness, make

For nearly eight years Rutger Hauer personified Guinness in Great Britain, and for the first time drinkers were shown the connection between Guinness and individuality; were shown that Guinness is good for your brain and mental strength.

Other 'Men with the Guinness' appeared around the world – George Lam in Singapore, Wenanty Nosul in Australia. The popularity of the 'Man with the Guinness' was shown in sales volumes.

In Africa advertising had always gone different ways. In 'The Traveller's Tale', we told some of the story of Guinness's growth in Africa from the 1960s onwards. When looking at the more recent history of Guinness in Africa we have to place David Hampshire at the centre of our story. And David played a particularly crucial role at one turning point for Guinness advertising in Africa.

David Hampshire had worked in Zambia, then in Cameroon when Guinness took over the operation in 1981. From a small share of the market then, and a predominantly lager-based business, Cameroon is now the sixth largest market for Guinness in the world.

d he fondly recounts Alan's friendly advice:

## it of money, have a bit of fun"

Africa is David Hampshire's continent

## He understands Africa and its diverse nation

The commitment he has shown, against the tide of opinion
for long periods, has grown the market for Guinness
phenomenally. In 1993 he became Managing Director
for the Africa region. And in 1997 he was faced with
a decision that made him swallow hard because so much
depended on it. Get it right and Guinness would prosper
throughout Africa. Get it wrong and Guinness would be
set back years.

It was clear that the fragmented approach to advertising
Guinness in Africa was leaving the brand vulnerable
to new, sophisticated competition. Was Guinness still
going to be relevant to the changing African market?
Was Guinness able to communicate enough passion
about its brand?

David Hampshire's concern was shared by Celia Couchman
who was the Marketing Director for Africa at that time.
Guinness advertising throughout the region looked tired.
A totally new approach was needed. A new agency, new
ideas, new challenges.

**To say that is easy, it's like an act
of bravura. Only if you really believe
it, can you deliver.**

## believes in Africa and its potential

Faced with a range of approaches from different ad agencies pitching for the work, David Hampshire and his team were attracted to what seemed a completely wild idea from Saatchi's, an agency that had no African location. The idea was wild, but intriguing. They wanted to see more. They invited Saatchi's to take it on to the next stage.

In David Hampshire's words:

## "They threw everything into it"

The wild idea was for a 'James Bond' character. It was scary even to contemplate because it was so risky, particularly in this market, to go for something so completely different. "When you've got 60% adorers" said David Hampshire, "that's not an opportunity, that's a responsibility."

The Saatchi execution was brilliantly put across. The Guinness team found themselves being convinced against all their expectations. The character as presented was Michael King.

David Hampshire suggested that he would be better with a slight name change, so Michael Power was brought to life through 3-minute adventures on TV and in cinemas, on billboards and print, through sporting endorsements. Michael Power has become an African hero of extraordinary reach and resonance, a figure of pride for African nations and for Guinness.

## Did it work? Of course it did!

The correct decision was the brave decision. The sales figures prove it. More Guinness is sold in Africa now than in Ireland.

## Only believe.

We've looked a lot at the past, not because we're so obsessed with history, definitely not because we want to wallow in nostalgia. But we can learn from the past, from the great people who have made our brand great. We can draw inner strength from them. We can admire the way they have come to a possible turning point and made the courageous choice which has turned out to be the effective choice.

We can use them as our inspirations as we look to the future and know that we will need to make courageous choices.

We need inner strength to do that.

**We have it**

Believe

The six stories were produced as a book. The original intention was to introduce the stories and the book at a global brand summit in late September 2001. But we had learnt that people and events shape history, so we had to be philosophical when September 11 led to the cancellation of the summit. However, everyone believed in the value of the stories to clarify the meaning of the brand for people involved with Guinness.

Alternative plans were made, and the book was distributed to the Guinness world. Not only that, the stories proved the inspiration for a video, a CD-ROM induction pack and a notebook. People understood the brand through the stories. They made vivid sense of the more conventional synthesis that had been written in 'brand-speak'. In simplified form the brand model looked like this:

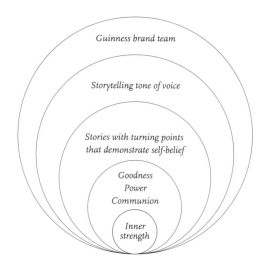

*Guinness brand team*

*Storytelling tone of voice*

*Stories with turning points that demonstrate self-belief*

*Goodness*
*Power*
*Communion*

*Inner strength*

The stories enabled people to understand and to remember what was really meant by the concept of inner strength. And, the challenge for any brand is to gain effortless recognition of and identification with its values. Stories are a powerful way to do so.

With Guinness I just happened to stumble upon the brand that provided the perfect example of harmony between inner and outer manifestations of the brand, an example that shows how storytelling becomes a 'tightrope between two worlds'. Here we have the inner world of the individual customer/drinker and the external world of communication and advertising that is the most overt representation of the brand. The Guinness stories provide the creative link between these two worlds. For those working with Guinness these stories offer tangible evidence of the truth of the relatively abstract brand definitions and descriptions. Without ever intending it in this way, the definition of Guinness as the brand of 'inner strength' became the natural platform for story-telling and for the brand's tone of voice. The possibilities are still being explored with Guinness as I write, but there is no question that a consistent tone of voice based on principles of storytelling, uniting internal and external communication, is an achievable aim.

### Stories to illuminate meaning

Soon after writing the Guinness stories, I was approached by the BBC. I was asked by David May, the BBC's head of strategic communications, to develop a workshop for his team, based on exploring the principles of storytelling. As we discussed what was needed, it became clear that we would also be exploring the BBC brand.

I decided to take a deliberately conventional version of a brand model:

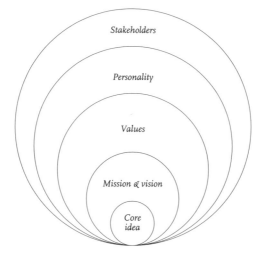

And see if this could equate to a storytelling model. Guinness provided a useful example to build on, and the following model emerged:

Here I am using 'stories' and 'narrative' with particular meanings, although often they are used interchangeably. In this model I use narrative as the overarching framework, the theme whose meaning the detailed stories will demonstrate. With Guinness, the narrative had been, 'How self-belief overcomes obstacles', and the stories told of six key turning points and the people who had been involved in them.

At this time too, soon after the attacks on New York's Twin Towers, Mario Cuomo was interviewed about the US response to the crisis. Probed by a BBC interviewer, he resisted the invitation to criticize President Bush.

**The President talks the tabloid headlines. Colin Powell follows on with the proper sentences and paragraphs.**

The overall message from Cuomo was: 'This works.' It's a good example of the way that modern communication needs to recognize the demands of the media while drawing on the most ancient of story-telling techniques. *Headline – story introduction – story expansion.* Read Homer, the world's oldest story-teller, and there's the same pattern. The *Iliad*, in the translation by Robert Fagles, begins:

**Rage – Goddess, sing the rage of Peleus' son Achilles, murderous, doomed, that cost the Achaeans countless losses, hurling down to the House of Death so many sturdy souls.**

If we remain with the form of epic poetry, then the narrative of Milton's *Paradise lost* is conveyed by its opening three lines:

**Of Mans First Disobedience, and the Fruit**
**Of that Forbidd'n Tree, whose mortal tast**
**Brought Death into the World, and all our woe.**

Milton then tells the stories that give meaning to this statement of the narrative.

This definition served me well for the BBC workshop. We explored ways of developing an overall narrative and using the skills of storytelling more effectively. The 'storytelling model' proved to be a viable alternative to the brand model, enabling us to look at the organization in a different and more personal way. The problem with the BBC (and its glory) is that it has a long history which is reflective of the nation's social history over the same period. If you live in the UK, there is a strong sense that the BBC is part of your life, that you 'own' it. That sense is breaking down as the competitive alternatives have opened up, but it is still a strong instinct within most British people. This makes the BBC an extraordinary brand but also a very difficult organization to change. For people working in the BBC there is a strange dilemma between the desire to be subversive and iconoclastic and the countervailing instinct to be cautious and conservative. The rational and the emotional constantly battle for supremacy.

This gave a certain tension to the workshop itself, and the storytelling model provided a means of resolving some of that tension. The exercises gave people permission to be iconoclastic through different kinds of storytelling, and they opened up meanings that might not previously have been apparent. One exercise was about writing a myth, as if it were an entry in an encyclopedia of Mythology. I gave each participant a different subject related to their area of job responsibility, and asked who might be the god or goddess to represent this subject. I thought the myth written by Andrew

Whyte was particularly good. So, Andrew, who was the god of strategy?

*Strategos was an artist who was charged by the Gods with painting The Big Picture – a visual representation of the whole creation.*

*It would be a long task because she had to visit everywhere in creation, look at it, understand it and then absorb its essential qualities in some way into The Big Picture. As it was such a huge task Strategos asked for help with the small but vital things she needed to make sure The Big Picture was achieved. To this end the Gods gave her an assistant to help: Tacticus.*

*But in reality Tacticus was a mixed blessing because although he was very good at his job sometimes he would lose sight of his contribution to The Big Picture and concentrate only on the task in hand. On occasion he would pay too much attention to the detail and lose the crucial sense of proportion of the whole.*

*Incubus was a minor God who didn't think The Big Picture mattered. It was distracting from the God's day-to-day core business, of playing with and tormenting mortals. So recognising Tacticus's tendency to be diverted by the short term he saw this as their main weakness and set about distracting them from their task, setting-up diversions by whispering absurd challenges in Tacticus's ear.*

In this case, the story/myth illuminates the meaning of strategy. It has a clarity and vividness that most writing about business strategy fails to achieve. The myths written by other participants were also able to shed fresh meaning on their roles within the organization. The challenge to re-express their roles within the form of a story liberated people from the normal corporate constraints. They were better able to let go, to take chances, to write in their own personalities.

I will conclude this chapter with one final example of a story that illuminates meaning, and that addresses the need to 'let go' that I have just alluded to. A recurring message of management consultants and business writers in recent years has been the need for people at work to release more of their innate creativity. Indeed, I have urged people to, 'Bring your personality to work'. Here is a similar message, expressed in the form of a story by Gordon MacKenzie from his wonderful book *Orbiting the giant hairball*.

*On my way to a conference in Stevens Point, Wisconsin, feeling a little hungry – it was near noon – I spotted an invitingly funky-looking roadside restaurant and pulled in. After ordering a cheeseburger and diet cola, I scanned, with idle interest, the floor-to-ceiling clutter of local memorabilia that served as interior décor.*

*Eventually, my wandering gaze carried me to two pool tables on the far side of the room beyond the eating area. One table was in use; the other was not. Beneath the vacant table, I saw a dog's legs. Standing. Still. I continued to scan the room, but with less interest than before. My eyes kept returning to the dog legs: still still.*

*My cheeseburger came. I ate without tasting. Distracted, transfixed really, by the motionless legs. I started feeling a little uneasy. Surely the dog was not stuffed . . . like the sad heads of moose and deer staring out from the café walls. That would be going too far. ('Strange,' I'd thought, 'Stuffed moose is okay; stuffed dog is not.') But the legs remained motionless.*

*How repugnant! A stuffed dog. I was regretting ever having entered such a grotesque establishment when, to my relief, the dog's tail moved – ever so slightly.*

*'Oh, good. I was mistaken. It's not a stuffed dog, after all. Just my imagination running rampant.'*

*The tail moved again, a subtle wag. Done eating, I could*

not leave without investigating what curious circumstances might keep this half-hidden dog standing still for so long. I paid my check and walked over to the other side of the pool tables.

Do you know how, along the side or end of some pool tables, there is a slot or trough where the balls go when they're sunk? Well, this dog had reached his mouth into the trough of the pool table and locked his jaws around one of the sunken balls. No way was he about to let go of his prize – but neither could he remove his mouth. His jaws, opened wide to accommodate the ball, were consequently opened too wide to allow him to escape from the confines of the trough. So there he stood, dead still, except for the now-and-then, hope-against-hope, wag of his tail.

I turned to the men absorbed in their play at the other table:

'Look at that dog!'

'Oh, he does that all the time,' responded one player.

'I've seen him stand like that for over an hour sometimes,' added the other.

'He wants someone to play with him.'

Poor dog. I left the restaurant feeling both sad for the mutt and fascinated by the lesson he'd provided:

If we do not let go, we make prisoners of ourselves.

To be fully free to create, we must first find the courage and willingness to let go:

Let go of the strategies that have worked for us in the past . . .

Let go of our biases, the foundations of our illusions . . .

Let go of our grievances, the root source of our victimhood . . .

Let go of our so-often-denied fear of being found unlovable.

You will find it is not a one-shot deal, this letting go. You must do it again and again and again. It's kind of like breathing. You can't breathe just once. Try it: Breathe just once. You'll pass out. If you stop letting go, your creative spirit will pass out.

*Now when I say let go, I do not mean reject. Because when you let go of something, it will still be there for you when you need it. But because you have stopped clinging, you will have freed yourself up to tap into other possibilities – possibilities that can help you deal with this world of accelerating change.*

Any business can draw meaning from that story. Each individual reading it will be thinking of their own role at work, their attitude to life. How do I go about my job? Am I like that dog? Or am I open to new suggestions? It raises questions and illuminates meaning simply because it is told as a story. When businesses and brands are seeking to communicate greater meaning to different audiences – internal audiences possibly even more than external ones – storytelling becomes a resource that needs to be taken more seriously. Brands – for increasingly businesses *are* brands – need to recruit as much as possible of the energy and creativity of their own workforces. Brands grow from the inside. They are then perceived from the outside by customers and other external audiences, but they will be found wanting if the inner spirit is weak. So brands need to give their own people not just permission but every encouragement to be creative within the framework of the brand's meaning. In that way they will create a far more engaging and effective message for their external audiences.

I find it illuminating to continue thinking about the BBC, not to point a critical finger but to see it as a beacon of hope. After the management consultancy style of the period when John Birt was director general, the new head of the BBC, Greg Dyke, felt the need to return the organization to its program-making roots. He talked about people who 'suck the oxygen out of ideas'. So a different culture was needed, a culture where cynics would not flourish, and where people would become more receptive to creative expression. No doubt storytelling is an important aspect of that, and who else told the story of the 20th century more compellingly than the BBC? The BBC World Service mission, engraved above the entrance of Bush House in London, remains stirring and motivating: 'And nation shall speak into nation.'

New ages need new versions of a story. In spring 2002 Greg Dyke told staff that his vision was for the BBC 'to be the most creative organization in the world'. Quite a difference, as he pointed out, from the Birt vision, 'to be the best-managed organization in the public sector'. But how will that vision be achieved? How will the still bland words that express the vision be given fresh life and meaning? Stories offer a way for all organizations to unlock and express their creativity. Perhaps, for the BBC and other brands, they point the way forward.

**Going underground** *'You must go on, I can't go on, I'll go on.'*
Samuel Beckett, *The unnameable*

# Underground writing

We reached a point at the end of the previous chapter where I suggested that storytelling and creative writing should be seen as more central to the business strategy and development of any organization. Of course, for many, this is almost a subversive thought. Such writing is like 'samizdat' publishing in the old Eastern bloc – those in control will suppress it because it is a threat to their continuing control. Safer, they believe, to allow corporate-speak and business jargon to flourish: it will not lead to any eruptions of emotion inside the organization.

Of course, I exaggerate. But two thoughts collided. The first was that I need to give practical help to those who, perhaps inspired by the storytelling potential explored in this book, wish to work on their writing skills. The second thought led on from 'subversive thought' to '"samizdat" publishing' to 'underground writing' – and the fact that traveling to and from work by London Underground, the Tube, is an important part of my life as a writer for people at work.

Growing up and living in London, I've always thought of the Tube as an extension of the public library system. Now, I know you can't actually borrow books from the Tube (although you can usually pick up a discarded newspaper or other reading matter). What you can do on the Tube, and what I've always enjoyed doing, is read.

Of all the books I've read in my life, I must have read at least a quarter of them on the Tube. You can open a book and lose yourself in the world of another mind, another place.

This has become even more essential to me since I began working and since my career started to involve more and more writing. Because reading and writing are, for me, two sides of the same coin. I know that reading helps writing. I wonder if writing helps reading. I believe it does.

Then it occurred to me that I had never tried to write while traveling on the Tube. I had written large sections of a book on planes and trains but the Tube had never seemed conducive to writing. Of course, it's often difficult to get a seat and standing up cramps anyone's writing style. But if you can get a seat . . . I wonder.

I became intrigued by the possibility. The more I thought about it, the more it related to my working life, and the more I thought I could relate to the working lives of my fellow commuters. After all, what are we all doing but traveling to work? My work involves writing. To some degree all our lives involve writing, or at least using words, and my purpose in life is to help people use words to greater effect and with greater enjoyment. Here, then, was an opportunity for different lines of thought to come together.

At this point in my thinking, I arrived at King's Cross, that great intersection of lines on the Tube map. The Tube itself could provide a metaphor for the chapter and perhaps even a structure. While working with London Underground the phrase, 'the fastest way to get from A to B' kept recurring. Now it suggested a useful discipline for the chapter that needed to be written, from A to B, B to C and on through 26 stations to Z, the end of the line.

The train pulled in to a different station (Leicester Square), a different thought arrived. A metaphor used by Howard Schultz, the man behind Starbucks, is that his coffee shops are 'the third place'. They're not home, they're not work, but they provide the bridge between home and work. I certainly like to collect a morning double espresso on my way in to the office but I'm convinced that for most Londoners the Tube is the real 'third place'. In other parts of the world there are other equivalents. The New York subway. The Paris Métro. Commuter trains in and out of all the world's cities. The bubble in which we journey to work is the real third place.

The problem is, the Tube is not nearly as comfortable or relaxing as a coffee bar. The best way to relax on the Tube is to read a book because that helps to blot out the surroundings. It's also, by the way, a wonderful lesson in the discipline of concentration.

So the whole idea formed to write this chapter *on* the Tube – and that's where these words were written. This is also a chapter *about* writing and storytelling. Perhaps I can help people to use words more effectively when they arrive at the 'second place', i.e. work? While each section might take me the duration of my Tube journey (11 stops) to *write*, each section might be *read* by a passenger between stops.

The only proper way to put this to the test was to hop on the Tube. I'm just pulling out of Gloucester Road station as I write this in my little notebook. I've cheated, but only a little, by starting to write on a Saturday rather than a workday. But from here onwards the chapter is going to be written between home and work on weekdays.

So the journey of the chapter has begun, another stage of the journey to find and show the Invisible Grail. We have discovered that stories can be a powerful resource for brands – but those stories need to be well told. This means going beyond the aspiration of 'Plain English' as *the* goal for business writing. As I sit in the carriage, pulling out of Green Park at this moment, the people around me seem to support at least part of my thesis. Of the ten people, two are reading newspapers, three are reading books, four

are lost in thought or in vacancy. Only one is writing. That one is me.

While I write, please read on.


**Getting to work**

**A to B** Any writer knows that it's not always easy to get started. Sometimes the world seems to be divided into writers and people who want to be writers. All of them might be struggling to get the first words down on the page.

Part of the problem is that oh-so-familiar phrase 'begin at the beginning.' I hate the phrase. Whoever first said it was probably a fundamentalist, but how did God begin? What was the story before the first day?

With any story, with any piece of writing, where is the real beginning? Realising the logical absurdity of the question, Laurence Sterne began his wonderfully absurd novel *Tristram Shandy* with the moment of his own conception.

> *Pray my dear, quoth my mother, have you forgot to wind up the clock? Good G\*\*!* **cried my father, making an exclamation, but taking care to moderate his voice at the same time, –** *Did ever woman, since the creation of the world, interrupt a man with such a silly question!* **Pray, what was your father saying? – Nothing.**

Begin at the beginning is impossible guidance. Sterne's joke is that his beginning was interrupted in the middle. My advice is 'begin in the middle.' Notice how different writers start their work. Learn from great writers. Apply what you learn to the words you use at work, whether you're writing a proposal, a letter, an email or a report. Plunging your reader

into the middle of things is the surest way to seize attention.

But care for your readers too. Having plunged them into deep water, help them by throwing them words that enable them to hold on to your meaning and to understand exactly where you and they are. There is a limit to the amount of surprise your reader can absor**b**.

**B to C**  Before you begin, think about how you'll best grab your reader's attention. Can you make a virtue of the fact that your reader hasn't a clue what you're going to write about? So, can you shock your reader into wanting to read on?

For example, how about this as the opening of a story?

**It was the year my mother stopped drinking, so it was two years after a careless driver killed my sister in a crosswalk, one year after my father died of a massive coronary on the front stairs, eight months before my brother Ronnie died of AIDS, and six months before he revealed his situation.**

That's the first paragraph of *Chris* by Edwina Portelle Romero, one of the *True tales of American life*, collected and edited by Paul Auster. I was intrigued by the idea of this book. It came about when Paul Auster appealed on National Public Radio for listeners to send in true stories about their lives. From the thousands sent in, many were read on air and 180 were published in *True tales*. It's a book that's a testament to the role of storytelling in all our lives.

There's a shock value in that opening paragraph. Deliberate, of course. Each of the individual tragedies in the paragraph might provide an introduction to seize attention. Put them all together and the effect is curious. You get the sense that this piling up of misfortunes is edging your emotions towards an ironic response.

Life, we're being shown, is full of random acts of unavoidable cruelty.

The fact is, your emotions need to be primed to respond to tragedy. Very few tragedies start with a death in the first scene. So be aware that your readers need to be taken on a journey with you; in time they might share the emotions you wish to arouse in them, but don't take that for granted.

Do you want to be crystal clear (here's what I'm going to tell you) or is puzzlement part of the effect you want to achieve (I want to intrigue you enough to carry on reading)? Remember – like the 'situation' referred to in that opening paragraph of Edwina Romero's story – it's only too easy, at the start of a piece of writing, to sound cryptic.

**C to D** Can you force yourself to think new thoughts and write new words by plunging yourself into a period of automatic writing? Who knows what will emerge when you allow one word to follow on from another in a stream you don't attempt to channel through any of the normal set ways of being. Being unconstrained is in a strange way a different form of constraint and from constraint you can burst free and unlock something surprising, something that had not previously occurred. Sitting on the Tube and writing is, it seems, the very place for random occurrences to happen along, for unbidden ideas to come whistling through a tunnel. Or perhaps to be held up by a signal and sent away back up the track, even if that turns out not to be the track you came down originally. Because you let your pencil write and it keeps moving and the only discipline you impose is a physical one to keep the pencil moving across the paper, not the mental discipline to shape your thoughts into conventional coherence. What emerges might be gibberish but it can help to release

your mind from the need to make absolute sense and to allow an essential element of chance and serendipity into your words. Because this word here might never have been placed next to that word there if we had thought longer about it, if it had been genuinely and deliberately placed instead of having emerged.

**D to E**    Do this, don't do that. Deadlines demand timely headlines. Alliteration and rhyme, the techniques of poetry, do we use them or abuse them? The Tube reminds us, through *Poems on the Underground*, that poetry can give us moments of meditation and inspiration in the most unlikely of settings – as we sit or stand on a crowded train, with a poem poster to read instead of an advert.

In the aftermath of September 11, President Bush – perhaps the least poetic president in US history – discovered the pitfalls and benefits of striving for uplifting language. 'We're gonna get these folks,' his immediate response to the crisis, was homespun but lacking in gravitas. So, perhaps stung by criticism, he plunged into longer words and deeper trouble. He emerged with 'crusade' and 'infinite justice', more rousing but offensive to Islam.

The president's speech to Congress (apparently written by his aide Michael Gerson) managed to reach a higher level. For example:

> **Our nation,**
> **this generation,**
> **will lift the dark threat of violence**
> **from our people and our future.**
> **We will rally the world to this cause**
> **by our efforts, by our courage.**
> **We will not tire.**
> **We will not falter**
> **And we will not fail.**

I have split the text into lines to emphasise the borrowing from poetry and rhetoric. Repetition, the deliberate use of repetition. Look at the last two lines where the alliteration in the double 'f' of 'falter' and 'fail' is accentuated by the half-rhyme contained in those two words. The echo of the first syllable of 'falter' allows the president, whether literally or metaphorically, to thump the podium on the last phrase.

**E to F**  Eggs over easy. Travelling to work in the morning, having just snatched a quick slice of toast, reminds me of that almost endless list of American ways of having eggs for breakfast. This then extends beyond the egg to varieties of pancake, waffle or bread. It becomes a litany of luxury, the list itself sending a message that implies, 'We have everything,' comfort food and a message of comfort for American culture.

Lists can be useful and they need not be boring. Some writers explore the way that lists can give vent to emotion. Günter Grass in *Dog years* runs the gamut of description involving 'brown', introducing into that list the spat-out 'Eva Braun' which works brilliantly in translation for needing no translation from the German.

But in business there is probably no technique used as boringly as the list. We've all sat in presentations where the next slide goes up and our hearts sink because it's yet another list, punctuated by bullet points.

In those cases the list is a lazy technique because the presenter is saying 'blah blah blah' in his mind in between points. Lists need connections. One word needs to lead to another. One thought needs to follow another. Start, think, stop, write, edit, think again. Listen to the rise and fall of the moving structure you're creating in this growing list, revise it, go back and add in new elements, question, ask yourself, 'What if?'

**F to G**   F\*\*\*. FCUK came along and the name dared you in the eyes. There has always been this divide between the words that you say in formal, public conversation and those that you say in private with your friends. But that gap has been disappearing over the years and now a game has developed where swear words are infiltrated knowingly into the public domain without being 'said'.

FCUK is one example of this development of expletive cheated. Another is 'BOGOF on holiday' where the BOGOF stands for 'Buy one, get one free' (of course). The important thing with expletive cheated is that you know the word that is not being said; the writer knows that you know; both reader and writer recognise that you are in this zone of public/private uncertainty, and the challenge is there to react with a smile of recognition (ah yes, I'm on that side of the fence) or with a snarl of disgust (whatever next?). The recent play that was listed as 'Shopping and f\*\*\*\*\*\*' drew good audiences of no doubt like-minded people, while a tiny minority would have been deterred from booking by having to speak the asterisks.

This is a language game that has been played for centuries (look back to the quote from Sterne in 'A to B' – By G\*\* ). It's a sign that the use of language is always about more than language. Language is a reflection and expression of changing social, cultural and moral debates, and all around us, through everyday language, we can hear and see those debates evolving.

**G to H**   Gotcha! Is the headline many British people think of when headlines are mentioned. It appeared on the front page of the *Sun* during the Falklands War when the British Navy sank the Argentinean ship, the *Belgrano*. At the time it reflected the sense of triumphalism that Margaret Thatcher had encouraged

in the nation when she had proclaimed her own headline ('Rejoice! Rejoice!') on the steps of Downing Street after British troops' first success in the war.

We live in a headline age. Business people, absorbed by their own busyness, demand: 'Just give me the headlines.' Of course we need to absorb information quickly and no one likes to waste time taking in unnecessary information. There's an art to writing the headline that will do the complete job: provide the reader with information and give your emotions a steer too.

It's an art, though, that is often abused. As I sit on the Tube this morning the *Sun* has another brilliant headline on its back page (sport). 'O'Teary,' it says, because the Leeds football team, managed by David O'Leary, crashed out of the UEFA Cup. I like that because it gives you fact and feeling in one headline. Because tabloid newspapers often do this well, people imitate it but sometimes imitate it badly. Open up most company newspapers and you'll find a whole rash of headlines containing bad imitations in the form of terrible puns.

For me, the pun in a headline should be a last resort. A pun rarely works when intended by the writer to be funny. It's easy to end up with the meaning being hijacked by the pun, rather than the pun expressing the real meaning. Good headlines are distillations of meaning in a few words. Concentrate on the meaning. Concentrate on the headline that will lead your reader most effectively to the story that will follow after. 'What a waste of life' says the *Daily Mail* today. It's 1 March 2002. Look up the story in the archives if you wish.

**H to I** How do you make a thought more vivid? Metaphors are certainly one way to do it. Look up metaphor in the dictionary and it will say something like 'figure of speech' which points out a resemblance between

things. Dictionaries can sometimes just raise another question about meaning. This might be one of those times when the dictionary definition makes sense only when you see an example. Indeed, a metaphor might be needed. The description of this book as a journey or a quest is a metaphor. The fact is we all use metaphors all the time, almost without realising, we use them as crutches, as shafts of light, as pointers, and they are certainly not confined to the language of poets. But often metaphors become clichés through overuse. Life is a . . . oh well, fill in your own response.

Writing this on the Tube reminds me of the Christopher Isherwood metaphor that opens *Goodbye to Berlin*: 'I am a camera with its shutter open . . .'

Over the last few days I've been working with different organisations on their 'brand platforms' (a metaphor itself). Different people from these different organisations have used metaphors to describe what each brand really stands for. One 'unlocks London'. The second is the 'bridge between considerate thinking and effective action'. The third is the 'treasure house of knowledge'. Three metaphors, not particularly original ones; but each manages to say more in fewer words than most of the alternatives raised in discussion. Our minds are surprisingly receptive to this allusive form of description. Plain words, factual descriptions, do not always communicate effectively because they fail to connect to the imagination.

Surely there is a lesson here for everyone who works. If you want to be more effective in the way you communicate with people at work, you need to tune in to their imaginations. Free your minds, use more metaphors, give greater rein to your audiences' thinking. Adopt the spirit of Billy Collins (see page 103). Allow your brain to waterski.

**I to J** I always prefer the first person pronouns 'I' and 'we' to their alternatives in the business world. The alternatives might be 'the corporation', 'the company', 'the organisation', 'the department' and so on. The alternatives are all relatively faceless but you could say they reflect the reality of business life. After all, Nokia communicates, IBM decides, London Underground apologises for the inconvenience caused, and it's New York State policy. Who am I to speak for them?

But my view is that if you're employed by a business you should be allowed, indeed encouraged, to write on behalf of that business as I or we. Perhaps some years ago this situation would have been different, but the times have changed and we (as consumers) now generally accept the convention that we (as employees) will write as real people.

The internet has given an extra push to the momentum that had been developing. Far from adding to the 'dehumanisation of business language' the internet has forced more and more companies to adopt conversational patterns of language, because the most effective communication on the internet is conducted as a dialogue. You are part of that dialogue and, unless you join in, the website will not work. So, we need to speak to you. I like it like that. It helps me to feel that I am dealing with a person not a group. Every company, every brand, is seen, heard, experienced through the individuals who represent it. There's no point in trying to hide those individuals behind a corporate screen.

In the same way I always warm more towards people who are personally welcoming in their names. The use of first names is now the norm in business. It's similar to feeling more attracted to the humanity inherent in a painting signed by Vincent rather than, say, RB Kitaj.

Just as English advances, other languages fight back. But the ground the other languages are fighting back on is increasingly English-held territory. The other day I bought a new pair of shoes, made in Portugal for Ecco, a Danish brand. The tiny leaflet that came with the shoes had information in four languages – Danish, English, German, French – under the title, 'Ecco – Shoes for life'. As I looked through the leaflet I noticed occasional English words like 'spray' in the Danish, as well as the heading, 'Product facts'. The German and French sections also used the headings, 'Shoes for life' and 'Product facts' – not, presumably, because these are concepts untranslatable into those languages but because an assumption is made that they will be generally understood. And because something attaches to the use of those English phrases that the shoe manufacturer wishes to be associated with – a sense that English is the global language that rises above the others.

As I approach Covent Garden, I'm looking forward to my morning cup of coffee. On my way from the Tube there's a Caffé Nero, which calls itself 'the Italian coffee company'. There the choice will go beyond espresso, latte and cappuccino to macchiato, ristretto and mocha, all served by a barista. We speak a generic language of coffee that has Italian roots but, pressured by Starbucks, now has global reach. But we pick and mix our languages as it takes our fancy. Today I think I'll choose between a pain au raisin and a croissant with my coffee. Am I feeling French today? Language flows like lava, driven by old habits, patterns and history, but also by accident, emotion and luck.

**K to L**    Kilimanjaro, Kyoto, K-2, K-9. Words that release different memories, mainly from childhood. Words that I had not been conscious of in recent times until I forced myself this morning to answer my own challenge: think of some words beginning with K. I could go on from here to explore the memories evoked by one of those words and it would become the starting point for a story.

Our imaginations are like sponges waiting for a little moisture to soften them into active use. Memory provides the moisture. It's hard to think of any imaginative writing that has not been sparked into being by memory. So my advice is simple for anyone wishing to practise writing skills. Follow the advice of Nabokov's title: *Speak memory.* Memory does not recognise writer's block, it flows, and your words can flow with it. Do we remember what really happened or are we just remembering what we think happened? Who knows? Remembering the past becomes a means of inventing the present and the future, and the only truth that matters is what seems to us to be true. Believe that you remember and you will.

**L to M**    Let's linger a while with the beguiling sounds of words. Words are vessels containing meaning – but ping the outside of the vessel and it suggests what might be inside. The first sentence above stretches out like a lazy afternoon with time to spare, gliding from one 'l' sound to another and softly sliding into 's' and 'w' sounds. The very word 'glide' I've just used almost glistens with oil as it slips into the sentence, just as 'slide' gently follows after. Perhaps they both need the sentence to end with a plop.

There are these words, of course, and plop is one of them, which imitate sounds. Sometimes they come in compounds to indicate a musical aspect of sound, as used in many a pop song. Splish splash, I was taking a

bath, while listening to the pitter-patter of the falling rain. We use such words to help us with descriptions. I remember watching a TV interview with the novelist Geoff Ryman who was asked about a particular sentence he'd just written in his book *Lust*. The sentence was: 'Barefoot, his wet feet made scrunching noises on the wet sand.' The interviewer asked him: 'Is the word 'scrunching' important?' Ryman replied: 'Oh yes. If it was just noises you wouldn't hear it.'

But although it's important to think of what we want readers to be hearing as well as seeing when we tell a story, I'm more interested in using the sounds of words to suggest meaning more subliminally. It's all a matter of listening. Hard sounds – 'd', 't', 'p' – are good for making hard, thumping points. Softer sounds – 's', 'z', 'l', 'w' – insinuate themselves more subtly into our senses, although 's' can also hiss with passionate sibilance. Clustering a collection of 'c' and 'k' sounds can make a staccato opening to kick open a conversation. But 'm' can be sensual – think how we use 'mmm' to indicate a coming tasty moment.

We need to learn to love listening, and to listen to the inner meaning of words lodged in the sounds that make them.

**M to N**    Messages are communicated through the words that we write. That message can be a simple instruction or a complex argument. But as well as the message about meaning, we are sending other messages through the way we write: signals about who we are, what we are like, about our attitude and personality. This represents the writer's tone of voice.

Literary critics often comment about a writer having a 'distinctive voice' or 'needing to find his own voice'. Writing for brands needs to be close to speaking, rather than a formal way of writing. Each of us has a

way of speaking that is distinctive. There are certain words or phrases that we use or avoid, there are personal patterns to our speech, we place emphasis on certain words or syllables, our accents shape the way we say things. This distinctiveness comes from the combination of influences that make us individual: our parents, schools, friends, where we live, what we do. Above all, what we believe as people, the values that underlie our behaviour.

It's no different for companies or brands except that we're talking about a collection of individuals rather than one person. But a brand, like an individual, has parentage, it lives in a context of ethical, educational, social influences. A brand's tone of voice springs out of its values. If these values are shared by the individuals who represent the brand – if not, what are you doing there? – then the individuals should share a tone of voice. That does not mean that everyone needs to write or speak the same, but that there should be a common framework shaped by the brand's values. Within this framework individuals can write in ways that express their own individuality. If they do so, their writing will be more engaging and more effective, and the brand will communicate better than if people are trying to put on a personality and style that is alien.

**N to O**  Nothing will come of nothing, as we know from *King Lear*. By this Lear means that his daughter Cordelia will get no part of the inheritance if she refuses to say what she believes will be false words. Of course, we're all on Cordelia's side. Her arguments are perfectly reasonable – how could she insist that her father was the sole focus of her love when she was about to marry a husband with her father's blessing?

Straight talking can get you into all sorts of problems. All Cordelia needed to do was flatter her father, use a

few fine phrases as her sisters had already done and, hey ho, the biggest part of the kingdom would be hers. But she balked at the fine words if she could not really mean them.

It might cost us, but honesty is the best policy. People imagine that brand consultants are trained to be economical with the truth. Far from it. Our job is to find the truth, then present it in a way that people will find most sympathy with.

When writing for a brand, straight talking pays dividends most of the time. Straight talking does not mean being rude or arrogant, but writing in a way that people will understand, really understand. Use the techniques I've been writing about in this chapter to tell the truth well. But it's not just about writing style: it's also about questioning the fundamental editorial principles behind a brand's writing. Don't hide behind the legal protection of disclaimers that force you towards innocuousness. After reading one bank's customer magazine, I noticed the small print that said:

> **This magazine is published as a customer service. The views expressed are those of individual contributors. Contributions published in this magazine are not intended to, and do not, represent professional advice on the subject matter dealt with. Where appropriate and necessary, professional advice should be sought.**

Why? Wouldn't it be a better, bolder, more interesting magazine if it restated its editorial policy as:

> **This magazine is published for our customers. We ask individuals to write and we value their individuality. They have something to say – something that**

**matters to them and to our customers – but they
are always personal views not Bank policy dictated
from above. We believe that liberates them to write
about subjects that interest them in ways that will
really interest our customers.**

Should the bank have changed its editorial policy?
Yes. Too few risks are taken in business and with
words. Did the bank change? No.

**O to P**     Once I gave a poem to a participant in a workshop. It
was this poem by William Carlos Williams:

**This is just to say**

**I have eaten
the plums
that were in
the icebox**

**and which
you were probably
saving
for breakfast**

**Forgive me
they were delicious
so sweet
and so cold**

The person I gave the poem to told me that she read
the poem every day after that. It became a morning tonic.
That was appropriate as Williams was a doctor who
used to write his poems on prescription pads in
between seeing patients. This explains the brevity as
well as the intensity of his poems.

Those are virtues to aim for. There is an assumption, though, that 'concise is good.' Sometimes we need to challenge that and say, 'precise is better.' If we are to be precise, often we'll need to use more words rather than fewer. I've come to hate the cop-out that frequently accompanies the use of the phrase 'less is more.' Minimalism in writing is rarely exciting, nearly always cold and uninvolving.

The real challenge is to use specific description well. 'Plums are good' is concise but not particularly interesting. 'I like the smooth skin of plums' tells you a bit more. The Williams poem tells you a lot more because it describes a scene and invites you into a situation through simple but precise description. Your imagination is then more than willing to colour in between the details, to flesh them out, to buff them up.

**P to Q** Punctuation is the cause of many problems non-writers know better than writers. Do they they do. There were periods in the 20th century when you needed to play with punctuation if you were to be considered a serious writer. Writers like James Joyce were interested in achieving a closer approximation of real thought processes through abandoning the normal rules of punctuation, to which Molly Bloom said yes yes yes. But something else happens that is interesting: new ambiguities are exposed through changes in punctuation. There's a pub-game example: 'woman without her man is nothing'. Add punctuation of your choice. Do all the women do this? 'Woman. Without her, man is nothing.' Do all the men fail to spot the possibility at all?

When writing for business, we need to be relatively strict about punctuation because a missed comma, full stop, apostrophe or question mark can change the meaning of what is read. Clarity needs to be a fundamental principle of business writing, even though we

might want to do so much more. Establish clarity first; in doing so, you might find that you have gone a step beyond clarity towards grace. You need considered punctuation to achieve either clarity or grace. And you might even end up playing with punctuation to reinforce meaning, when you find yourself backed into a crowd and wanting to get out of the **q** . . .

**Q to R**    Questions can be very useful in helping you get started on a piece of writing. Why should this be so? Aren't questions inevitably a sign of some uncertainty? What if we want to give the impression that we are totally in control of our case? Relax. You can still be in control because the process of raising questions leads you to provide answers. But why are you so desperate to appear in control anyway? The whole process of thinking something through with questions and answers is one that happens in our minds constantly.

Questions can be used as important turning points in any narrative or presentation. *But what do we need to do at this point?* The question means that the reader or listener joins you in thinking your thoughts. *What would I do in this situation?*

Of course, there are many different ways of asking a question. You can be aggressive or gently curious. When working with Lever Fabergé I was interested in what happened when I turned dry descriptions of new concepts from the factual language of market research into a whole series of questions – and nothing but questions. One question led to another, forming a trail of enquiry that seemed to me to have the effect of being far more respectful to the 'target consumer'.

Did it work? Did it create a new way of writing concepts? No, but that was not the intention. The intention was simply to open people's minds to a

different possibility. And that is an important aim for any writer.

**R to S**  Rise to your feet and feel the words coursing through your veins. Sometimes it's no bad thing to stand on the Tube to read. You need to let words sing in your head and then you must dance along with them. The train rattles along the track; the words clatter inside your head in a matching rhythm. When reading we respond to sound and rhythm, even if we don't consciously acknowledge it. I'm a slow reader but a musical one. Words have their rhythm. Why rush them?

Tim Smit, founder of the amazing Eden Project in Cornwall, came to our office last night. He talked about catching the spirit of the samba jellyfish and using samba dancing as part of the induction for new people joining Eden. The samba jellyfish is a creature we can imitate in our childhood, but then it swims away out of our being. I wish I could dance. But I can in my head. And my words can dance straight off the page.

Some sentences have an easy lilt to them. When you write, your words can always be beautifully spoken in your head. You depend on no one else for their delivery. But you can give prompt cues to help your readers perform them as you would wish. Sway to high notes and low. Sometimes you can keep a steady rhythm swirling along but then, with a finger-snap, break it. We're talking of dance where earlier we talked of sound and song. Now the words are not just heard inside your head but felt inside your body. Mix short quick steps with languorous, slower, stretching ones.

**S to T**   Short simple words are the demands of the modern chief executive. Short words suit swift actions. Simple words fit clear decisions. But it can be a boring, monotonous diet for those having to take these words in.

That's why I value the occasional idiosyncratic word that can be like a slice of ginger in boiled rice. We need to savour words. I'm not advocating a return to Victorian propensities towards mellifluous concoctions of verbal superfluity. Let's simply aim for variety – but not of the *Good old days* kind, which used to recreate Victorian music hall linguistic excesses on the television of my childhood.

One relatively neglected way of doing this is through the use of compound words. English seems to have become less and less fond of these words as we have moved further from the language's Germanic and Anglo-Saxon roots. One of the features of the earliest English poetry is the regular use of words like whaleroad as a figurative description of the sea. Words like meadhall, marsh-den, warcry, chainmail seem to emerge through Celtic mists. In those days they used to unlock their wordhoard in order to speak.

Let's not forget that we also have access to a word-hoard and we need not use it for archaic purposes. Watergate has ever since inspired an endless succession of scandalgates. In a similar vein, 'I can't believe it's not butter', a name said breathlessly as one word, still has a distinctive soundring a decade after its introduction. It seems to me clearly in the tradition of Mr Bedonebyasyoudid and Mrs Doasyouwouldbedoneby in *The Water Babies*. These are inventions which linger in the memory. Perhaps we need to pursue this kind of verbal invention more frequently if we're to achieve what we might call mindlift.

**T to U**   Talking in someone else's voice is a kind of impressionism that has nothing to do with Monet. Ironically, since I have been writing about finding your own tone of voice, let me suggest an exercise that aims to do that by casting off your own voice altogether.

In *We, me, them & it* I wrote about 'letting your twin brother have all the laughs'. A writer develops a persona that is close to their real self but is different in that it is a writer's persona. It exists slightly outside the person. Often you get a strange feeling reading something you have written and you ask yourself: 'Did I really write that?' I'm eerily aware, even as I write these words, that the same question will face me some months on from here as I read them in a different time and place.

An exercise that has, at the very least, caused a lot of fun in workshops, is to get people to write a letter in the tone of voice of a celebrity personality. Decide what the subject is going to be for the whole group: let's say a reply to a letter of complaint from a customer. Then assign a different personality to each of the participants: George W Bush, Tony Blair, Woody Allen, Oprah Winfrey, Michael Moore. The letters written in response to this challenge show how perceptive people are and how easily understandable the whole concept of tone of voice is.

What it also does, when you then turn back to your own tone of voice, is to send you back with greater confidence to the kinds of words and phrases that are really you.

**U to V**   Usually adverts come one at a time. At Covent Garden tube station for the last two weeks, we've had a rash of big Orange posters. Across the tracks from the platform, there has been a complete vista of adverts for the mobile phone company. The ads show photographs of 'ordinary people' of different ages living their own lifestyles, and different colloquial phrases come from

the mouths of the people in the shots. The phrases are, in this order as you walk the length of the platform: oy oy, Eh up lad, yo, 'ello 'ello 'ello, eh-oh, wotcha, hi, 'ello chuck.

The message is that Orange is for everyone. So they've chosen colloquial English to get that across. I dislike the adverts but it's not because of the use of everyday phrases. It's just that the use seems a little patronising in this case.

That's the danger of using the vernacular in your communication messages. It's very easy to hit a slightly off note. But the fact is that we're surrounded by everyday slang, code and street-talk, and most of that language has an energy and inventiveness that helps to refresh our view of life. Phrases like 'sorted' enter the mainstream. Marks & Spencer as the representative of middle England slipped effortlessly into a poster that simply said 'Chill'.

The entertainment media are the fast channels for distribution of the new colloquialism. This week was announced as G-DAY which means there is a new movie out, with Ali G as the star who both imitates and spreads the language of cool rap. There's a hint of the Australian everyday greeting too ('G'day'), so we see colloquialisms crossing national and cultural borders with knowing ease.

The phrase 'dumbing down' has been used a lot lately by the culturally conservative who seem to me to misinterpret much of modern life, especially its pleasures. The BBC has certainly been a target of the dumbing-down attack. But last night I laughed myself silly watching Billy Connolly, the big yin, on BBC TV. His language is rich, dirty and colloquial, and he commentates sharply on the way we all use language. He had particular fun with the phrase, 'there's a bug going round'. He also came out with the following: 'That's what happens to songwriters when they die. They decompose.' Dumbing down has a long way to go before it's reality.

The tube train's at Covent Garden and I'm back to the reality of a platform full of Orange ads. Not a patch on Billy Connolly. We all sign off colloquially these days. 'Yours sincerely' is decomposing, replaced by 'LOL' in text form or simply 'luv'.

**V to W**  Very few of you will have read this far and failed to notice that I like to use quotations. I like them for their own sake, because someone has said something enlightening, true or amusing, and also because they become part of the narrative argument. I see them a bit like the interchange stations on the Tube. They allow you to continue your journey, while taking a short break, then heading off in a different direction.

> **Eternity's a terrible thought. I mean, where's it going to end?**
> Tom Stoppard, *Rosenkrantz and Guildenstern are dead*

Other people see quotations as big landmarks, perceptions that you should stand and stare at in awe, opportunities to think about life, death and eternity, reflections to capture in a picture frame on the wall. I remember as a child being given for a school prize *Arthur Mee's book of everlasting things*. This weighty book came from the Victorian tradition of expecting culture to shape our moral sensibility. Take a great painting three times a day, an uplifting quotation with your breakfast and afternoon tea, and a classical story in the evening after dinner. I'm less keen on these landmark quotations which are meant to give you guidance on life itself.

Abraham Lincoln, though, wanted just such a quotation to give him regular sustenance. Apparently he admired some words that had been created for an Eastern potentate: 'And this too shall pass away.'

Lincoln cherished those words because you can read them in good times or bad. In times of triumph they would damp down pride. In times of affliction they would provide solace.

'I buy that' as the quotation might go, if it wasn't said by everyone. We demand individuality and memorability from our quotations. But when you use them, use them to advance your argument not to put them in a picture frame. People need to see each quotation in a context that seems new.

**W to X**   'What's in a name?' goes the over-familiar quotation from *Romeo and Juliet*. Obviously quite a lot as a name is the basis for our identities as individuals, brands or organisations. And then there is the UK's once-revered Post Office. Would a rose named Consignia smell as sweet? It might, but the new Consignia didn't have the same goodwill attached to it as the old Post Office, and the Consignia chairman was regretting this name change to his business within months of it happening.

The problem was that the name Post Office was invested with centuries of stories. Few brands have that kind of heritage. Although the reasons for the change were perfectly rational in a business context – this was a change to the holding company name, the name Post Office could not be registered for use internationally, the technological context in which the business operated had changed dramatically etc, etc – these reasons were scorned aside by an emotional response from the general public. The public were saying we know the Post Office as a symbol of something good that we have valued and whose passing we regret. Everyone knew personal stories that were based around the idea of the Post Office at the heart of local communities. Here was a new name, Consignia, which removed the experience from the individual and local to the impersonal and international.

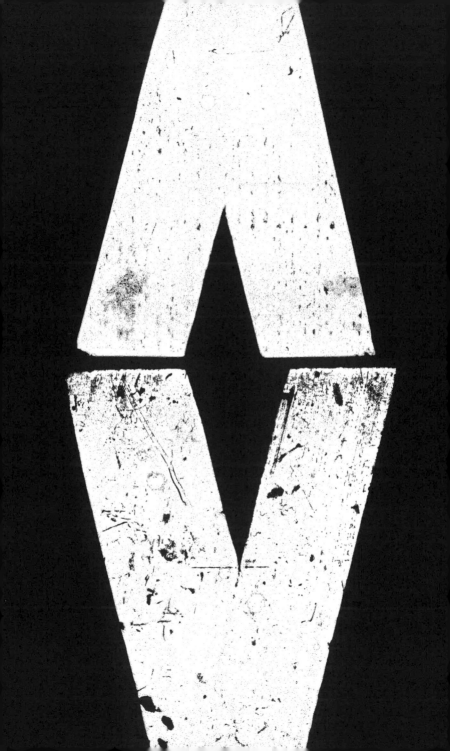

But that was the strategy. Had the strategy been thought through? Had the rational been weighed properly against the emotional? When it comes to a name the emotional counts for a lot. Think of the emotion we put into naming a child. Naming a business or brand can involve emotion too, much as we try to approach it through a rational, strategic viewpoint.

So in the end that gut feeling really matters. *I like/hate that name.* Brands are increasingly driven by business and legal necessities towards manufactured names. The need to register domain names on the internet has added enormous complexity to the whole challenge. There are good solutions: Google, for example, suggests the spirit of searching and serendipity which drives the internet. There are also questionable solutions, many of them found to be good after deeper questioning, many based on Latinate inventions or rare letter combinations and sounding like high-scoring words in a game of Scrabble: Xerox, Uniq, Zaviva.

Actually that proves another point. You can get used to any name over time. Don't reject new names out of hand, you might just grow to love them. Many copiers followed after Xerox.

**X to Y**     Xerxes is a favourite name from my childhood reading. My imagination was stirred by tales of the ancient world. Perhaps that's why I quite like Xerox: it reminds me, deep down, of an almost legendary figure.

We all have favourite words as well as favourite names. In workshops I often ask people to think what their favourite word might be. This was spurred by a survey a year or two ago, which aimed to find out 'the nation's favourite word'. Bob Geldof launched it on a website and, some months and thousands of votes later, 'serendipity' was announced as the winner. I've probably used that word a few times in this book but I'm not

sure if I would have done ten years ago. Which reminds me that I really like 'probably'.

This survey forced me to think of my own favourite word. I voted for 'Blimey' because it's a word with good memories from my childhood (an early example of expletive cheated too). I like Blimey because you say it to express frustration but, having said it, there's no chance of any anger developing. It just makes you smile because actually you know it's quite silly.

My colleague Mark Griffiths voted for 'Gravy' for his own reasons. I then came across a poem by Raymond Carver that seemed to support his case for gravy to be seen as a word meaning something special. Now he keeps the poem called *Gravy* on his desk.

The first line is:

**No other word will do. For that's what it was. Gravy.**

Serendipity. Probably. Gravy. What can I say? Does every favourite word end in 'y'? Why?

Blimey.

**Y to Z**   You have been with me on this underground point-to-point outing for something like 25 steps now. So you know that we're nearing the end. And you've probably guessed that there's only one subject to end with: endings.

Each piece of writing needs its own properly considered ending. Endings are probably more important than openings because they really are the last word, and you won't have a next sentence to come to your rescue if you get it wrong. What I have discovered by writing this series of pieces with fixed constraints – i.e. start with a word beginning with 'y' and finish with a word ending with 'z' – is that such discipline forces you to see each piece of writing as complete in itself. Think of everything you write as needing to have this same sense of

completeness: you need to craft it, chisel it, shape it until it feels naturally complete. Because writing is thinking, it is a thought rather than just a technique that provides the completeness. *Good endings need a resonant thought.* That thought can be underscored by a technical detail: end in 'z', use alliteration, use balancing clauses. The rhyming couplet to close a scene in a play is a formal example:

> **Cheerly to sea; the signs of war advance.**
> **No King of England, if not King of France.**
> William Shakespeare, *Henry V*

Perhaps all good endings have a feeling of inevitability about them too. We might not have known exactly where we were heading but it feels right once we are there. Each day provides us with a new journey; so does each new piece of writing. We need to approach each journey as a voyage of discovery every bit as personally momentous as when Columbus embarked on a tiny ship and set sail for a new world. What is waiting there for us? Think how the world was about to change when Columbus headed westwards from Cadiz.

**Journey's end** '*The real voyage of discovery lies not in seeking new landscapes but in having new eyes.*'
Marcel Proust

6

# Endings and beginnings

*What did I expect to find? Mr Kurtz at the end of the Piccadilly line? The horror, the horror. No, my expectations are always more optimistic.*

We've come a long way in pursuit of our quest and we have seen many things. We have asked many questions and suggested answers to them. We set out to find what, by reason, had to be there. But perhaps it was like the country or continent or even planet not yet charted on our map. It seemed invisible, but we believed it had to exist. Or perhaps what we were looking for could not be seen because it was too obvious although it was there all the time, staring us in the face. Or perhaps, like the specters in a story, we could not see them until we were ready to see them.

To see the grail you need to want to see it. Brands, both big and small, want to find a closer engagement with customers and other audiences, globally and locally. Brands need to discover, or rediscover, the words to do that. Is the grail then to do with language itself, or more particularly to do with the use of the English language? Yes, but we have needed to go further. Is the grail to do with developing connections between the brand and its customers through the way language is used to engage in conversations? Yes, but we have still needed to go further.

Is the grail about creating a more emotional link, at a deeper archetypal level, through the use of stories? Do these stories connect not just with external audiences – customers – but even more powerfully with internal audiences? We have seen this certainly, but we have seen that we have needed to go a step beyond this to complete the quest. Because, having discovered the value of stories, these stories need to be told well, they have to use language with love and belief. This means going beyond the basics of good business writing to a form of creative writing for business. All these questions are linked, as inevitably are the answers.

This is the challenge for our times, to see and accept that brands engage effectively only when they use all the elements of identity as well as they have learnt to use the visual elements. There was a time when businesses understood, almost as a flash of divine revelation, that using a symbol or logo consistently would not just help people to recognize them but would also create a bond of belief and loyalty between them. It took a while for this to become obvious despite the evidence of the world's religions using exactly the same visual methods for centuries. The cross of Christianity is one example, but other religions provide other examples.

But, in the beginning was the word. If religions have pioneered the use of visual symbolism to inform, communicate and reinforce belief, they have relied on language even more to spread their message. Language and all its tools of trade: ringing phrases, parables, prayers, mantras, poetry, evocative names, stories.

Rabbi Jonathan Sacks wrote the following in an article:

**At the heart of any culture is the process by which we bring successive generations into a narrative, the story of which we are a part. There is, of course, not one story but many, but storytelling is the place where identity is found, it is the vehicle of community ...**
**Stories tell us who we are, where we come from and what we might aspire to be. A culture is defined by its narratives.**

He was leading to a point about television and its responsibility for upholding narrative within the cultures of all modern societies. Television is vitally important. So too are businesses, and the brands that represent businesses. And there is, in any case, a synergy between the media and brands, with each reinforcing the other. We can see brands as mirrors and shapers of cultures, as well as vessels that contain beliefs. So they need stories.

Stories are at the heart of any culture, every system of belief. They are the way we share what we have in common. They are the way we understand another person's philosophy, to embrace it or reject it. They create links between people and they build bridges between different minds and different worlds.

So this then is the grail that is now visible. We seek ways for brands to engage more closely with people, both at a global and local level. Here is the way to create that grail, to give it more substance, to ensure its visibility. It involves language itself, but it goes deeper than that, to a language that creates connections and conversations with customers, employees and all audiences. It uses the potential of language to tell stories that reach people emotionally, and it sets standards for the use of language that rise above the primary ambition of clarity. It means using words emotively, expressively, engagingly. It means telling stories.

Of course, many will say, we've always known that; and it is true that most, including most business people, will under the slightest pressure acknowledge that the ability to use words is a crucial skill in life. They might then go on to say, with a self-deprecating laugh, 'but I'm not very good with them myself.' At the same time, these same people are reading books, articles, editions of management consultancy journals to find something new that will give their business a competitive advantage. How many books on business re-engineering, for example, are particularly well written? Should it not be explained well? What will be the next fashionable business concept? Will it need to use words to describe itself? Will it use words well?

I am not arguing that words are an unknown business resource, simply that they are a poorly used, misunderstood and neglected resource. This is why they are the invisible grail. It is like a company discovering that it has a vast undervalued property portfolio. At different times in business history words come into greater prominence. The example of Anthony Trollope's reports on the Victorian postal service shows that there have been moments when greater value was placed on the quality of writing for business. The fact that Port Sunlight still plays a living part in the development of Unilever shows that the good deeds of brand founders continue to provide narrative resonance through different generations. But we ignore or forget these lessons every so often. This book is an attempt to discover some of these truths afresh so that we can see them again with a clarity that we can apply to business, brands and ourselves today.

It does come down to *ourselves*. I'm always aware, indeed reassured, that books are read by individuals and not by organizations. The impetus for change has to come from individuals deciding that this is something that they have the power and the desire to act upon. The action might then lead to changes within a business or a brand but it begins with one person making a resolution. The resolution to give more time and thought to writing is actually an easier one than most personal or business resolutions. 'I'm going to change this company's business processes' is a resolution that might call for a higher level of collaborative effort and persuasion. 'I'm going to write better' starts with *you*. But it could continue with the business or the brand you work for.

Are brands starting to see the potential of creative writing? I was first intrigued, then disappointed, by the fact that Fay Weldon's last novel was sponsored by Bulgari. I was intrigued because it seemed like an example of a brand recognizing the importance of creative writing; then disappointed because it turned out to be more like a rather cynical piece of product placement. More interesting is the website provided by Orange to track the writing of a historical novel by Kate Mosse. The Orange Labyrinth website (www.orangelabyrinth.co.uk) seeks to engage readers and writers in a community that will share experiences of these activities. Kate Mosse was also the person behind the creation of the Orange prize for fiction by women writers. What's in it for Orange? Perhaps, most interestingly, simply the association with creative writing and a brave assertion that Orange believes fictional writing matters. For me that seems an intelligent example of brand development. Others might not agree, particularly when set beside the facts and figures that show that – by comparison – a certain kind of business remodelxing will definitely lead to an increase in shareholder value. We are not encouraged to bring an emotional, romantic belief in creativity into the rational arena of running a business.

Yet many people are now doing just this. The tide might just be on the turn and there are some signs of the turning tide in this book. So think of the opportunities to discover the potential in your company, in particular the creative force of words. Both the words you use within your own four walls and those you send outside. But who is going to use these words? Who is going to tell the stories? At the moment there might be no one doing that job. Some brands – as we have seen – have done it instinctively without giving anyone the job description 'storytelling'. Companies are only too happy to appoint a new conference organizer or a bought ledger clerk. But someone who is just going to find and write the brand's stories? What do you mean?

I see the time coming when companies will employ creative writers – for that's what I'm talking about, not communication managers, not people who will control a process. To do this will need a leap of faith because the company will need to invite the writer to write whatever he or she finds and feels is true to the brand. But think about the possibilities. Often creative writers are themselves brands who invoke tremendous brand loyalty in readers. These worlds are not that separate. In Victorian times people bought and read the new Charles Dickens, then queued to witness the live performance. Today, literary festivals, readings in bookshops and writing events attract dedicated followers of authors like Ian Rankin, Barbara Kingsolver, Nick Hornby, John Irving. Brands should not try to buy such authors for themselves, they should try to develop their own writers who will bring creative ideas into the everyday business environment. And those writers should also develop creative writing skills throughout the business.

I am not talking about an explosion of writers-in-residence (much as I like the concept of the writer-in-residence). I am suggesting a more fundamental change to the ways companies and brands develop their own distinctive stories. Call it an experiment, call it an act of faith. Some experiments work, some do not, but risk-taking is an essential element of business life.

Being a writer changes a person. You might change not just one person but every person in your workforce. It seems to me that there is nothing to be lost if that happens and everything to be gained. My personal belief is that 'I think therefore I write. I write therefore I think.' The activities of thinking and writing are inextricable for me, and by trying to become better writers we become better thinkers. As we have seen on the journey, a company gains much by taking steps to improve its writing ability. But more, even, than we have seen, it gains a group of individuals who are better able to deal with the challenges that the business will throw at them.

Thinking you're a writer changes you too. Lord Longford, campaigner for lost causes, forever standing up for the underdog, wrote a book that he called *Humility*. It was ironic, then, that one day soon after the book's publication he stormed into a bookshop demanding to know why it was not in the shop window.

There's the danger for you. What might you be unleashing? A tempest of humility, a hurricane of opinion, a storm of stories? Will they be good or bad stories? You'll want them to be good ones, and the chances are, they will be. Have faith and you will discover something worth knowing. That is almost the creed of the writer faced with a blank sheet of paper. Believe me, I've been there, I go there every day.

Tails '*Where is the writer when the reader is reading?*'
Margaret Atwood, *Negotiating with the dead*

# Reading

Reading and writing are two sides of the same coin. The best way to refresh your writing is to refresh your reading. Great books are a constant source of inspiration for any writer; what you read inevitably influences what you write. So here are the ten books that influenced me most while conceiving and writing this book. I hope you'll be equally refreshed by them.

> **Restoration** *by* Rose Tremain, a beautifully written novel set in the time of Charles II that confronts you intriguingly with the question, 'Where is the beginning?'

> **The Poisonwood Bible** *by* Barbara Kingsolver, the story of a missionary family in the Congo in the 1960s, told through the different views and voices of the female members of the family. Think about 'tone of voice' and read Adah's tale.

> **New York trilogy** *by* Paul Auster, intriguing mystery stories about identity and about being a writer.

> **Atonement** *by* Ian McEwan, an intensely moving novel which tells a wonderful story that also happens to be an exploration of the act of writing.

> **A prayer for Owen Meany** *by* John Irving, the book on this list that I feel most evangelical about. It made me laugh out loud for its humor and weep in public for its sadness. Read it, it's extraordinary.

**My year of meat** *by* Ruth L Oseki, a novel about the meat trade and cultural differences. Constantly surprising, an unlikely good read.

**An instance of the fingerpost** *by* Ian Pears, a historical novel that tells the same story from four different viewpoints and leaves you wondering about the nature of truth.

**English passengers** *by* Matthew Kneale, which won the Booker Prize and uses many voices wonderfully well.

**His dark materials** trilogy *by* Philip Pullman, supposedly written for children but perhaps even more disturbing for adults in its exploration of good and evil, life and death. These books are like rediscovering the absolute essence of epic storytelling, in a line from Homer, Virgil, Milton and onwards.

Those are nine works of fiction. I read and learnt something from each of them. There is a misconception that we learn most from works of non-fiction. In fact we learn from books that are well written, fiction or non-fiction. My tenth book is the only 'business book' on the list.

**Orbiting the giant hairball** *by* Gordon MacKenzie, the 'creative paradox' of Hallmark Cards, who wrote this, the most readable and inspiring book I've ever read about working in the corporate world.

## Acknowledgments

I would like to thank the following for the use of extracts reproduced in this book. 'She being Brand' is reprinted from *Complete poems 1904–1962* by E. E. Cummings, edited by George J. Firmage, by permission of W.W.Norton & Company. Copyright © 1991 by the Trustees for the E. E. Cummings Trust and George James Firmage. 'Chris' by Edwina Portelle Romero from *True tales of American life*, edited by Paul Auster, published by Faber & Faber. 'This is just to say' by William Carlos Williams, from *Collected poems*, published by Carcanet Press Limited. 'O' from *Eunoia* by Christian Bok, published by Coach House Books. 'Introduction to poctry' by Billy Collins, from *The apple that astonished Paris*, copyright 1988, reprinted by permission of the University of Arkansas Press. 'Story' by Steve Denning from *The springboard*, published by Butterworth-Heinemann Business Books. *Orbiting the giant hairball* by Gordon MacKenzie, copyright 1996, published by Viking Penguin. 'The moon's a golf course' by Jackie Wills, copyright 2001. 'Strategos' by Andrew Whyte. Strenuous efforts have been made to contact all copyright holders and we apologize if any have been inadvertently overlooked.

## Photo credits

Jessie Simmons *pages 9, 36, 37, 38, 67, 88, 90, 91, 94, 96*
Action Images *page 19*
Innocent Drinks *pages 57, 59, 61, 64*

# Index

## About TEXERE

TEXERE seeks to become the most progressive and authoritative voice in business publishing by cultivating and enhancing ideas that will illuminate the global business landscape. Our name defines the spirit of our vision: TEXERE is the ancient Latin verb 'to weave'. In an increasingly global business community, we seek to create an intersection where authors and readers can share the best thinking and the latest ideas. We want to leverage the expertise and insights of leading thinkers by weaving them with TEXERE's capability to deliver them to the marketplace. To learn more and become a part of our community visit us at: www.etexere.com and www.etexere.co.uk

## About the typefaces

This book was set in FF Scala and Parisine Bold. The FF Scala typeface was created in the late 1990's by the Dutch designer Martin Majoor. Majoor is recognized for his success in redesigning the Dutch telephone books. French designer Jean-Françoise Porchez created the Parisine typeface in 1996 for signage on the Paris Metro network.